AF263702

The Square Book

of

Savannah Squares

Photography by Megan Jones
Poetry by Christopher Soucy

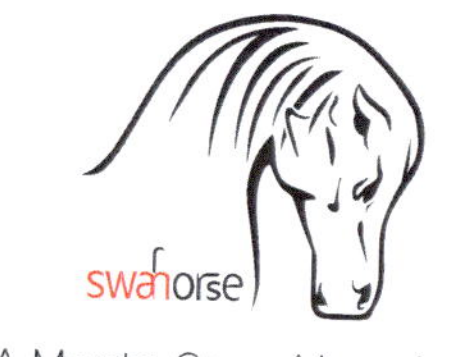

A Monte Ceceri Imprint

THE SQUARE BOOK
OF SAVANNAH SQUARES

Epigraph from James Edward Oglethorpe's "An Appeal for the Georgia Colony," *London Journal*, July 29, 1732, reprinted in Rodney M. Baine, ed., *Publications of James Edward Oglethorpe* (Athens: University of Georgia Press, 1994), 160.

Vintage frames and background designed by starline: Freepik.com (https://www.freepik.com/free-vector/classic-white-vintage-frames-stickers_17819759.htm)

ISBN 978-1-949512-11-3

1. Photobooks. 2. Poetry. 3. Savannah (Ga.)—Nonfiction. 4. Illustrated works—Photobooks. 5. United States—Nonfiction. I. Title

For information about special orders, press inquiries, or appearances or speaking requests, please contact Monte Ceceri Publishers.

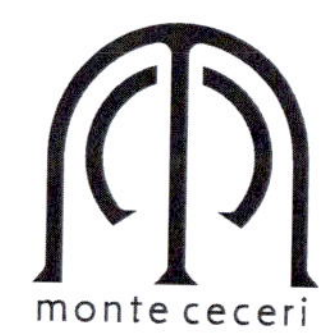

Monte Ceceri Publishers
P. O. Box 60623
Savannah, GA 31420
www.montececeri.com

A City so sensible of what was right, so touched with the Miseries of their Fellow-Creatures, could not fail of Success; they were worthy of the Empire of the World.

—James Edward Oglethorpe
"An Appeal for the Georgia Colony"
London Journal, July 29, 1732

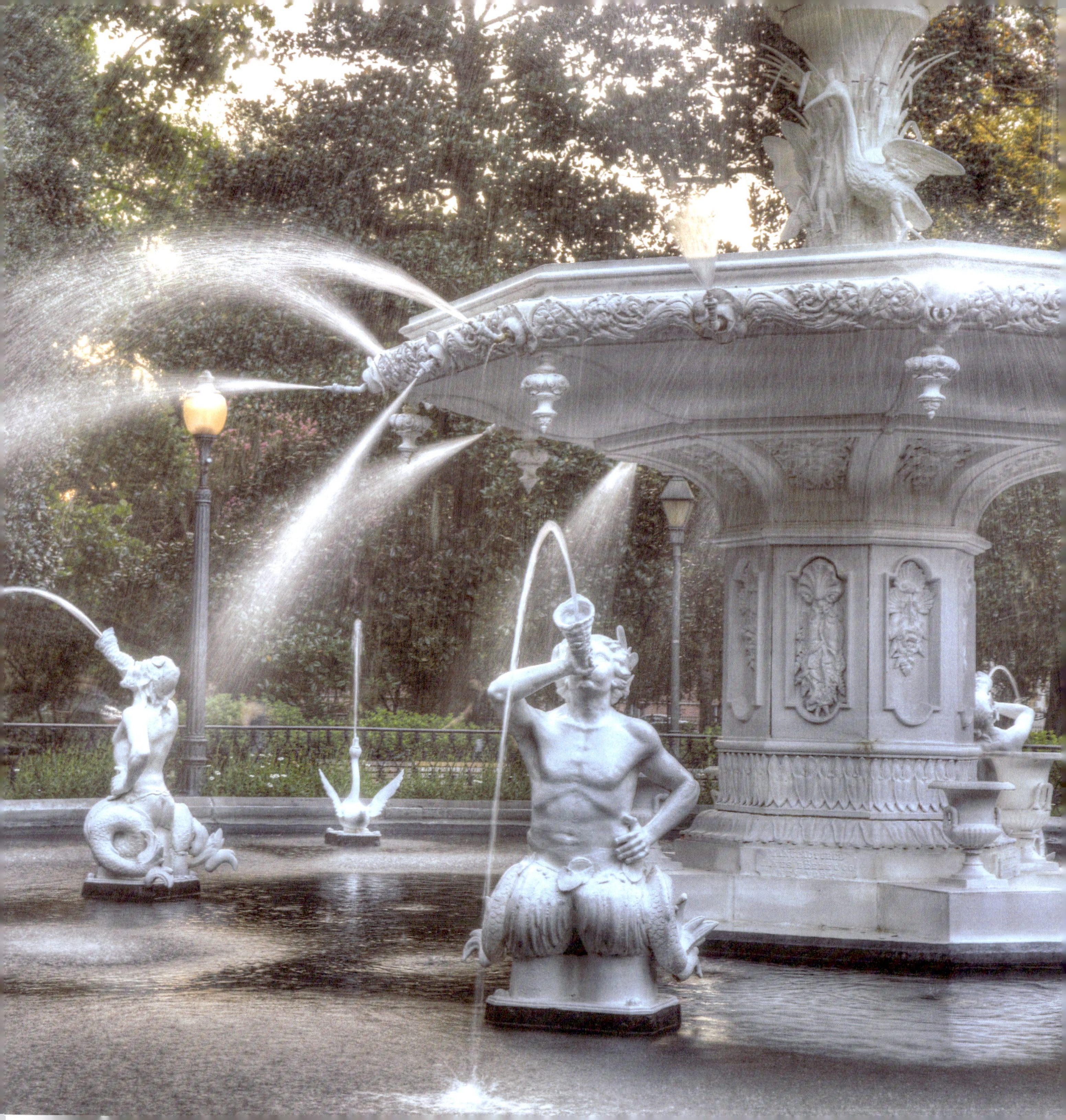

In November 1732, more than one hundred passengers set sail from Gravesend on the River Thames for a two-month journey aboard the vessel *Anne* and destined for territory near Charles Town, South Carolina. James Edward Oglethorpe — a member of Parliament with humanitarian ideas in mind — traveled with them in order "to direct the first operations for establishing [a] new colony."[1] Until this time, "New Georgia" had been home to several Native American nations and was considered by the English to be a part of the Carolinas, but the province and city that Oglethorpe was to found would (at least initially) be distinct in both name and approach.

Born in 1696, Oglethorpe was an Enlightenment-era Londoner who attended Eton and Oxford, serving briefly in military campaigns in between. Though privileged, he championed social reforms during his time in Parliament and as colonial governor of Georgia. He advocated for better conditions for sailors in the Royal Navy as well as for prison reform — especially in light of the harsh debtors' laws that devastated individuals and families at the time.[2] In fact, Robert Castell, an architect and friend of Oglethorpe's, died of smallpox in 1729 while serving such a sentence in Fleet Prison. This personal connection not only influenced Oglethorpe's progressive efforts but also likely his vision for Savannah.[3]

After leading a parliamentary committee investigating the British prison system, "Oglethorpe and his group of like-minded reformers determined that the blank slate of an American colony would be a more viable approach to providing the worthy poor with a place to begin life anew."[4]

The Trustees for the new "Colony of Georgia in America" had three main objectives: to develop a military stronghold against the competing interests of the Spanish and the French; to create an agrarian laboratory to produce crops and goods for export back to England; and to secure via "practical philanthropy"[5] a self-sustaining "utopia that would provide new opportunities for debtors, promote equality by limiting the size of the tracts provided to the settlers, tolerate religious differences, utilize the most advanced contemporary approaches to agriculture, and prohibit slavery."[6]

It was to this third aim that Oglethorpe remained most wedded, and his enchanting design for the city of Savannah endures as a civic, architectural, and historical jewel of the United States.

Built on a bluff, "Savannah holds a unique place" in the annals of city planning.[7] The town itself overlooks the Savannah River, separating its residential region from both the narrow waterfront that was allocated as the city's commercial area and the "swamps which had given Charleston a reputation for being unhealthy."[8] Oglethorpe strategically claimed the indispensable waterway for the Hostess City of the South and prohibited rum and slavery. He directed a fort to be built as well as a "Beacon upon Tybee for to direct Ships on their making Land."[9] He established faithful trade relations with the various tribal nations.

But the heart of the Oglethorpe Plan prioritized the everyday lives of the residents, who would come together increasingly from different backgrounds. Oglethorpe designed Savannah "on the basis of a unit which could be repeated again and again as the town grew"[10] — "a co-ordinated system of repeated squares"[11] that at once echoed the "ideal cities" of the Renaissance and envisioned a more democratic future.[12]

Though such a utopia grew from ethnocentric assumptions and would be decimated by the blight of slavery two decades later, Oglethorpe's squares of Savannah held promise.

Beginning with six and quadrupling to twenty-four by 1851 — plus the addition of Forsyth Park and Colonial Park Cemetery — four squares would be lost in the modern era to the automobile and the needs of twentieth-century "progress." Two have since been reclaimed, including Ellis Square, whose antebellum history as the site of a slave market is a stark reminder of our past and a sobering lesson for our present and future. Another also has been renamed to honor the achievements and legacy of Susie King Taylor, a teacher, nurse, and writer who was born into slavery but prevailed in the face of such adversity and dedicated her life to improving that of others.

Some squares bear the names of presidents and Revolutionary War heroes, some the remains of those upon whose lives Savannah is built — whether Tomochichi, chief of the mighty Yamacraw nation; Andrew Bryan, founder of the First African Baptist Church; or Savannahians both enslaved and free.

Today, twenty-two squares as well as expanded versions of Colonial Cemetery and Forsyth remain.

No matter the era, Savannah continues to entice and enchant — even if it boasts certain incommodities that those from the *Anne* quickly discovered. As Thomas Causton wrote in a letter to his wife:

> Our Situation is indeed very pleasant, and tho' we want for nothing we have some Grumbletonians here also.... Last Christmas Day was the hottest day I ever felt in my Life being then in the Latitude of 19 Degrees. We have very heavy Rains sometimes but tho' it rains a whole Day and Night it makes no Dirt. We are much pestered with a little Fly they call a Sand Fly. I have seen it in England about the Horse Dung. But every Insect here is stronger than in England. The Ants are half an inch long and they say will bite desperately. As for Alligators I have seen several but they are by the Sides of Rivers, Our Town is too high Ground for them to Clamber up.... I find the Camphire very good against the Stings of the Flies. I now begin to be something hardened against them.[13]

The Oglethorpe Plan "made this Georgia colonial city one of America's urban gems,"[14] and as Frederic Stevenson has phrased it, in its squares "the very life of this town has been fostered and to imagine Savannah without them would be to imagine it without its soul."[15]

1   From an article reprinted in *The Georgia Historical Quarterly*, "An Early Description of Georgia: From the *Gentleman's Magazine*, January, 1756. Volume 26," *The Georgia Historical Quarterly* 2, no. 1 (March 1918): 37–42, 38.

2   Rodney M. Baine, ed., *Publications of James Edward Oglethorpe* (Athens: University of Georgia Press, 1994).

3   Turpin C. Bannister, "Oglethorpe's Sources for the Savannah Plan," *Journal of the Society of Architectural Historians* 20, no. 2 (May 1961): 47–62.

4   Roy H. Lopata, review of *The Oglethorpe Plan: Enlightenment Design in Savannah and Beyond*, by Thomas D. Wilson, *The Public Historian* 35, no. 2 (May 2013): 115–116, 116.

5   Frederic R. Stevenson, "Charleston and Savannah," *Journal of the Society of Architectural Historians* 10, no. 4 (December 1951): 3–9, 7.

6   Lopata, review of *The Oglethorpe Plan*, 116.

7   Bannister, "Oglethorpe's Sources for the Savannah Plan," 47.

8   Stevenson, "Charleston and Savannah," 7.

9   Letter from James Oglethorpe to the Trustees, September 17, 1733, reprinted in Kenneth Coleman and Milton Ready, eds., *Original Papers, Correspondence to The Trustees, James Oglethorpe, and Others, 1732-1735*, vol. 20, Colonial Records of the State of Georgia (Athens: University of Georgia Press, 1982), 35.

10 Stevenson, "Charleston and Savannah," 6.

11 Bannister, "Oglethorpe's Sources for the Savannah Plan," 56.

12 Stevenson, "Charleston and Savannah," 7.

13 Letter from Thomas Causton to his wife, March 12, 1732/3, reprinted in Coleman and Ready, *Original Papers, Correspondence to The Trustees, James Oglethorpe, and Others, 1732-1735*, 17–18.

14 Lopata, review of *The Oglethorpe Plan*, 115.

15 Stevenson, "Charleston and Savannah," 9.

·SAVANNAH·

- Established 1733 -

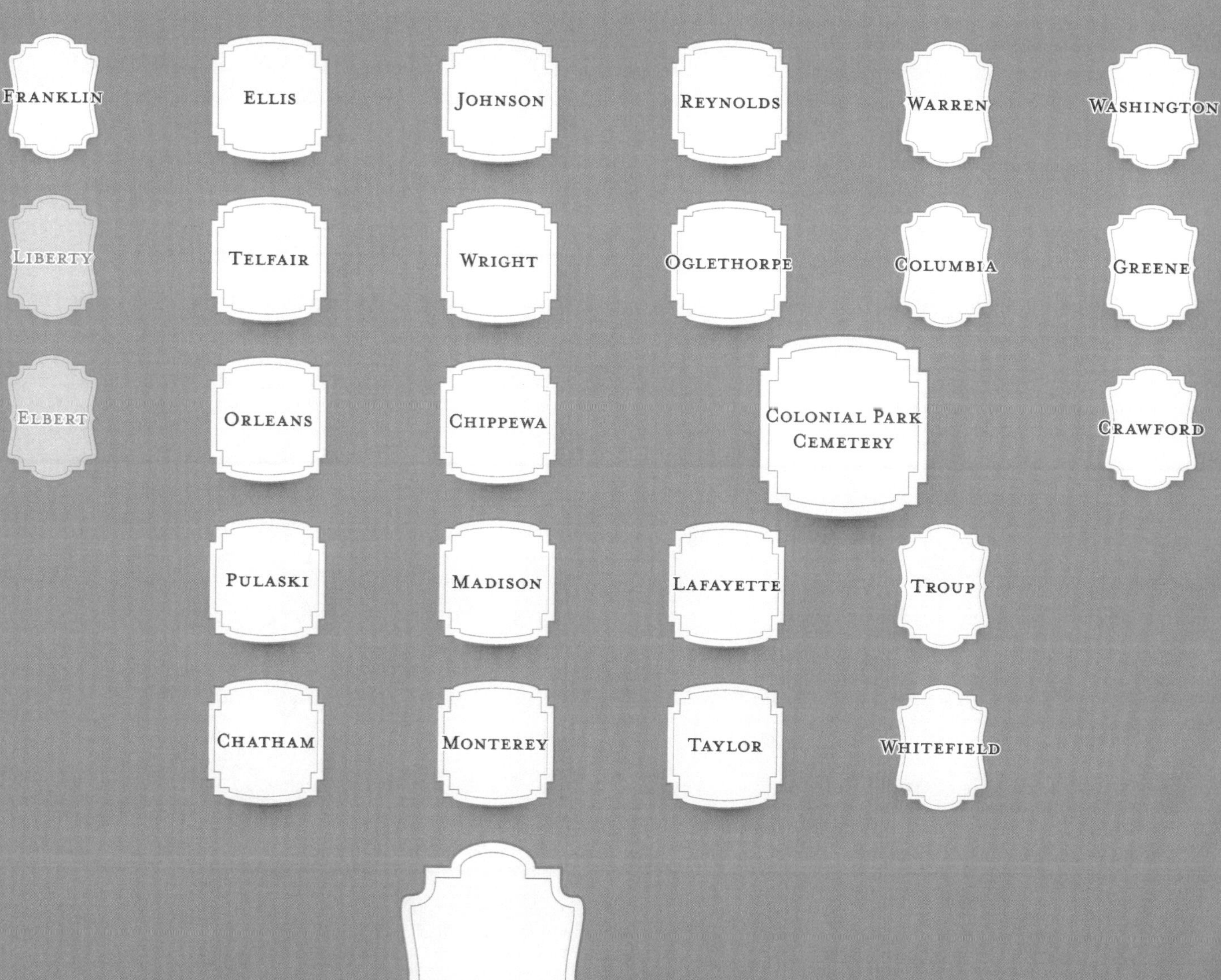

One morning I went for a little walk,
About the city, through its measure of squares.
With me I carried a caisson of chalk,
I desired to draw things that no one dares.

I sought inspiration to the left and the right,
I looked for a muse high above and below,
I looked and looked and looked day and night,
Nothing but silence, it troubled me so.

At last a vision forged in my mind,
I drew with a fury I never knew,
I used every color, every hue I could find,
From the deepest red to the coolest blue.

My masterpiece nearly drove me insane,
It lasted but briefly, until the next rain.

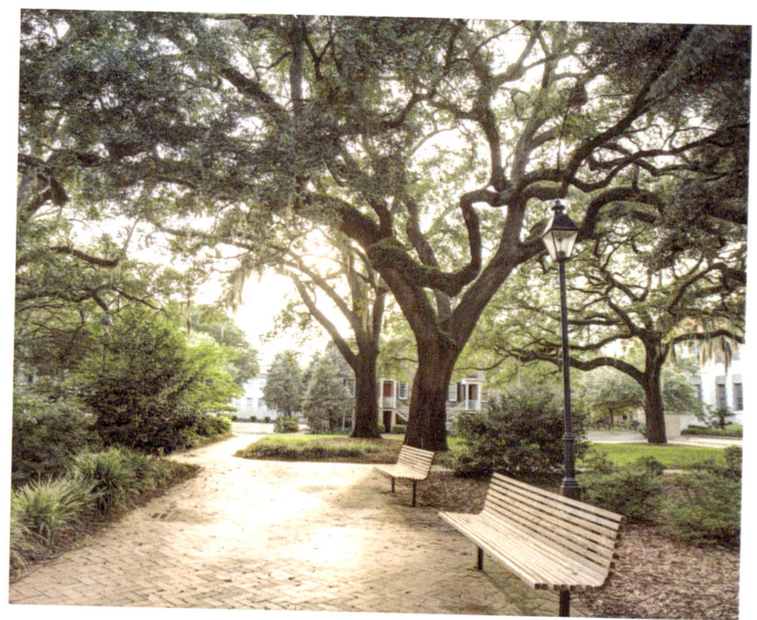

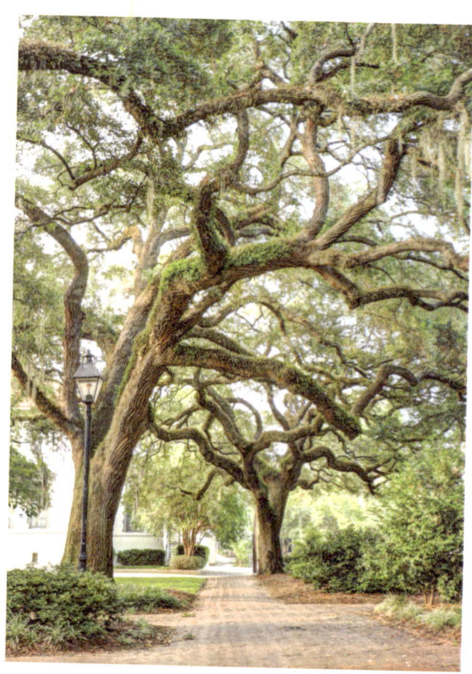

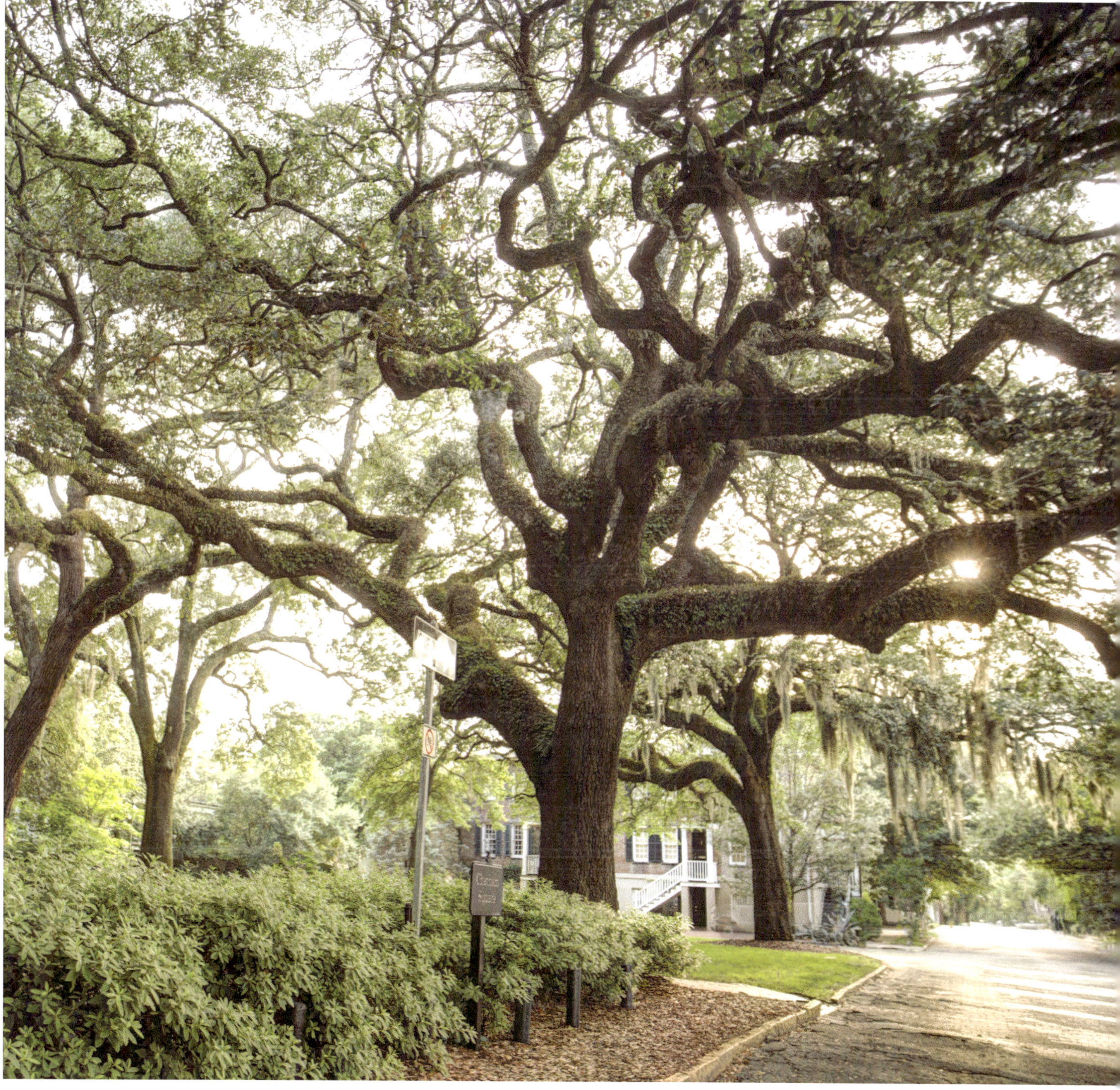

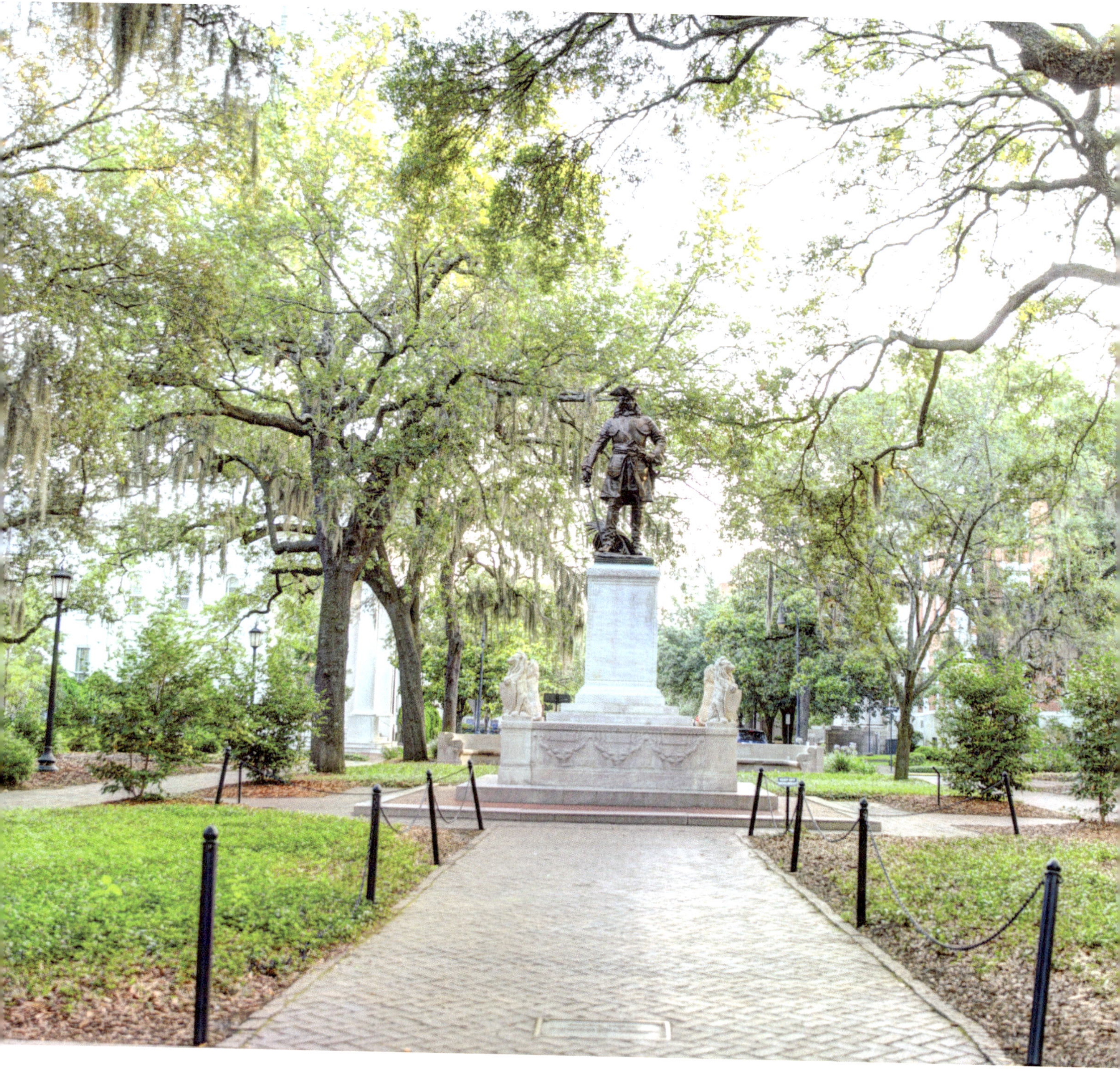

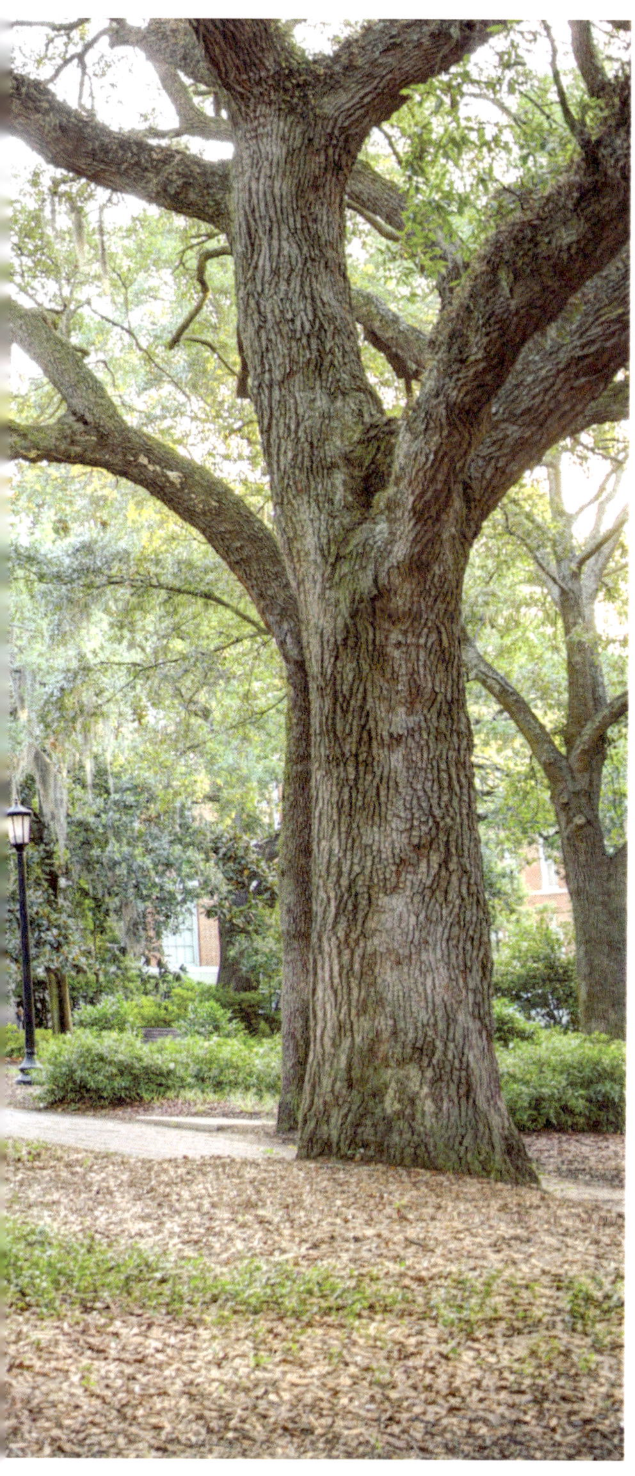

Chippewa Square

Standing still at the center of the square,
Holding my breath as the years slowly burn,
Come and stand in my view, in this place, if you dare,
And help me parley the respect that you've earned.

A tribute I pay to the passing of time,
Prepare I must do to fathom the past,
Every good deed and indeed every crime,
Flows and then ebbs from my view very fast.

I cannot be swayed, dare not even try,
My duty forever is carved in the stone,
None can escape from a watery eye,
Or be unfazed how the years have thus flown.

Statues are anchored and rarely retired,
But always applaud being praised and admired.

Columbia Square

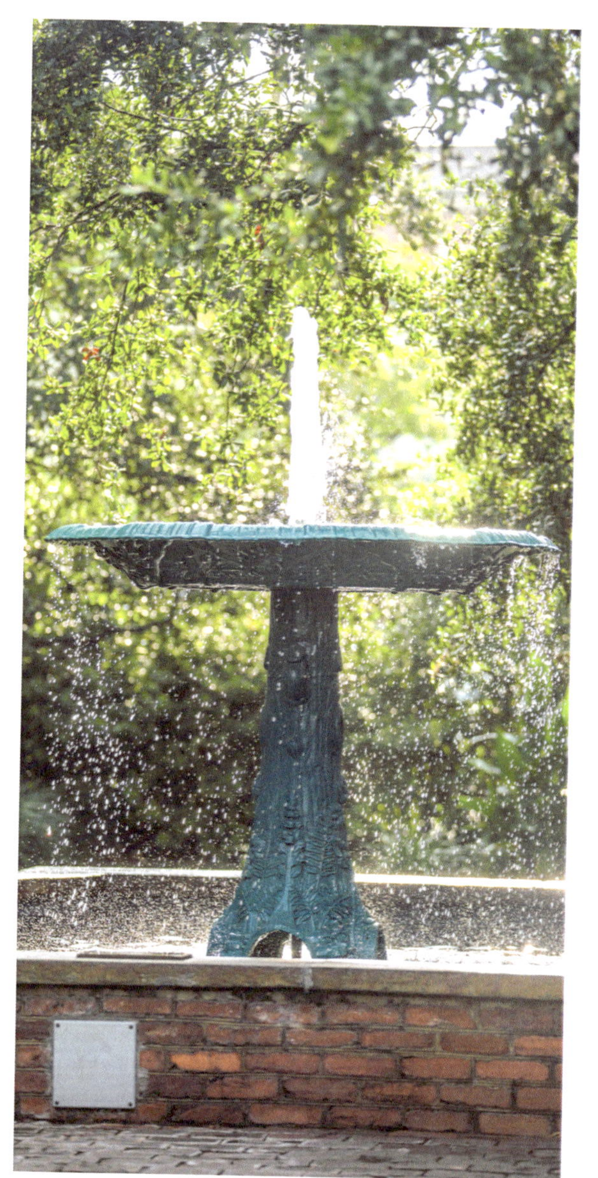

People who dream about falling in love
Often envision a fantastical place:
Nature's beauty she rides on sunlight above,
Essential to life as the eyes to the face.

A small kiss of warmth and caresses of green,
The amorous mood is perfectly set.
Nothing amiss in this mise-en-scène,
A moment like this one can never forget.

Imagine strolling the stage, hand laid in hand,
Breathing such sighs of contented relief;
There is a sweet scent reigning the land,
An ideal joy that transcends belief.

Not every place is the playhouse of dreams,
Though some settings surpass even sun-driven beams.

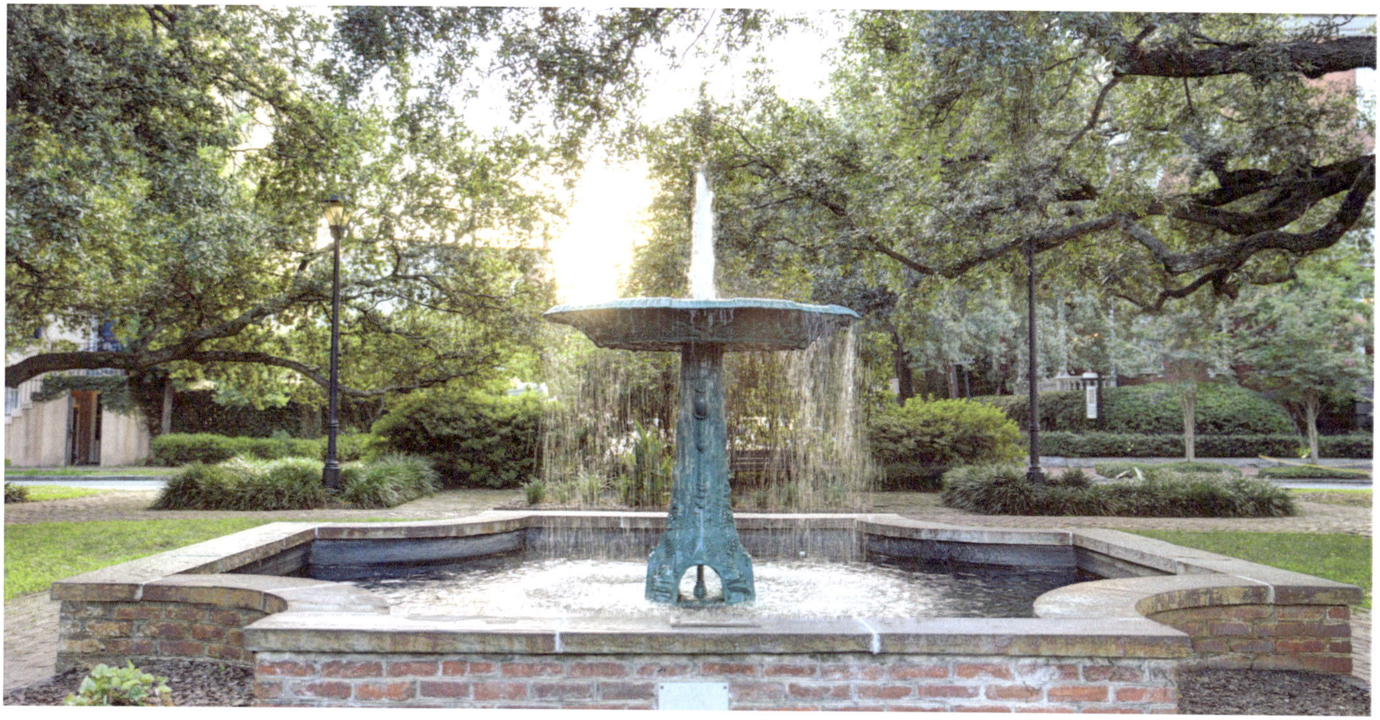

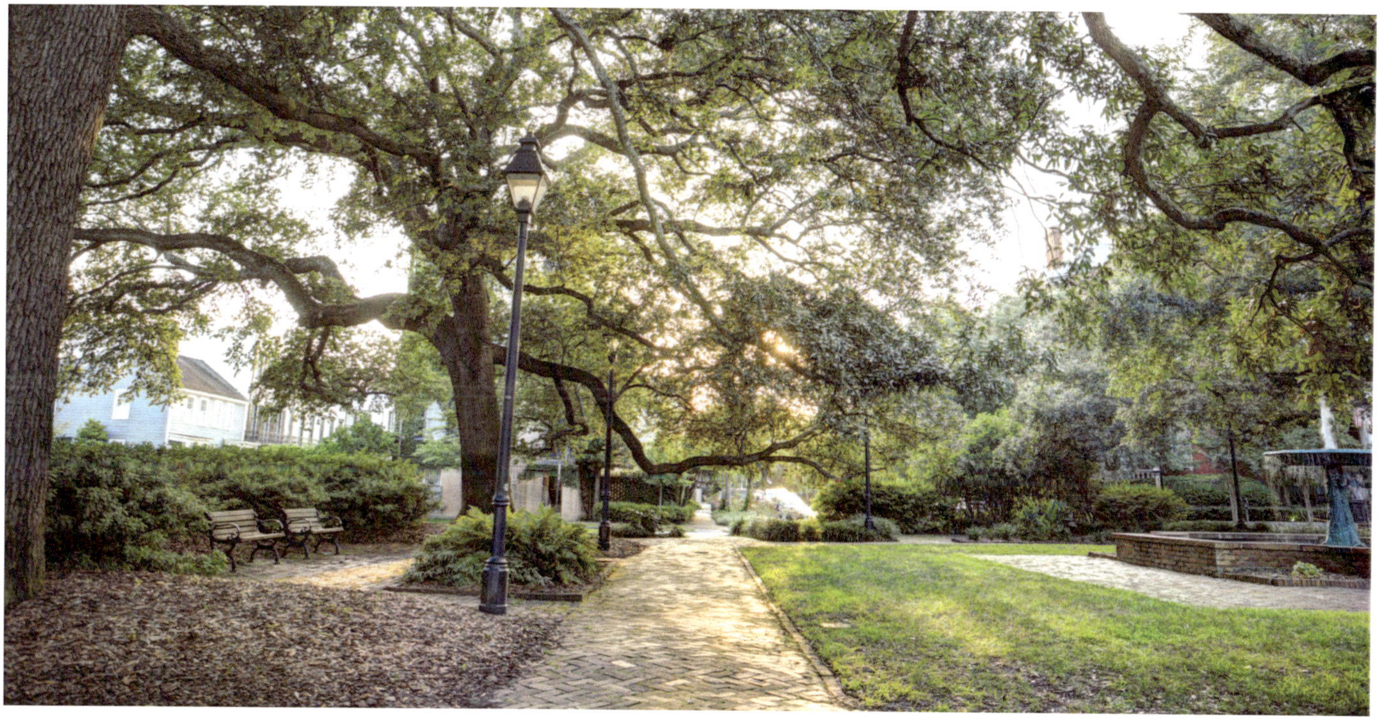

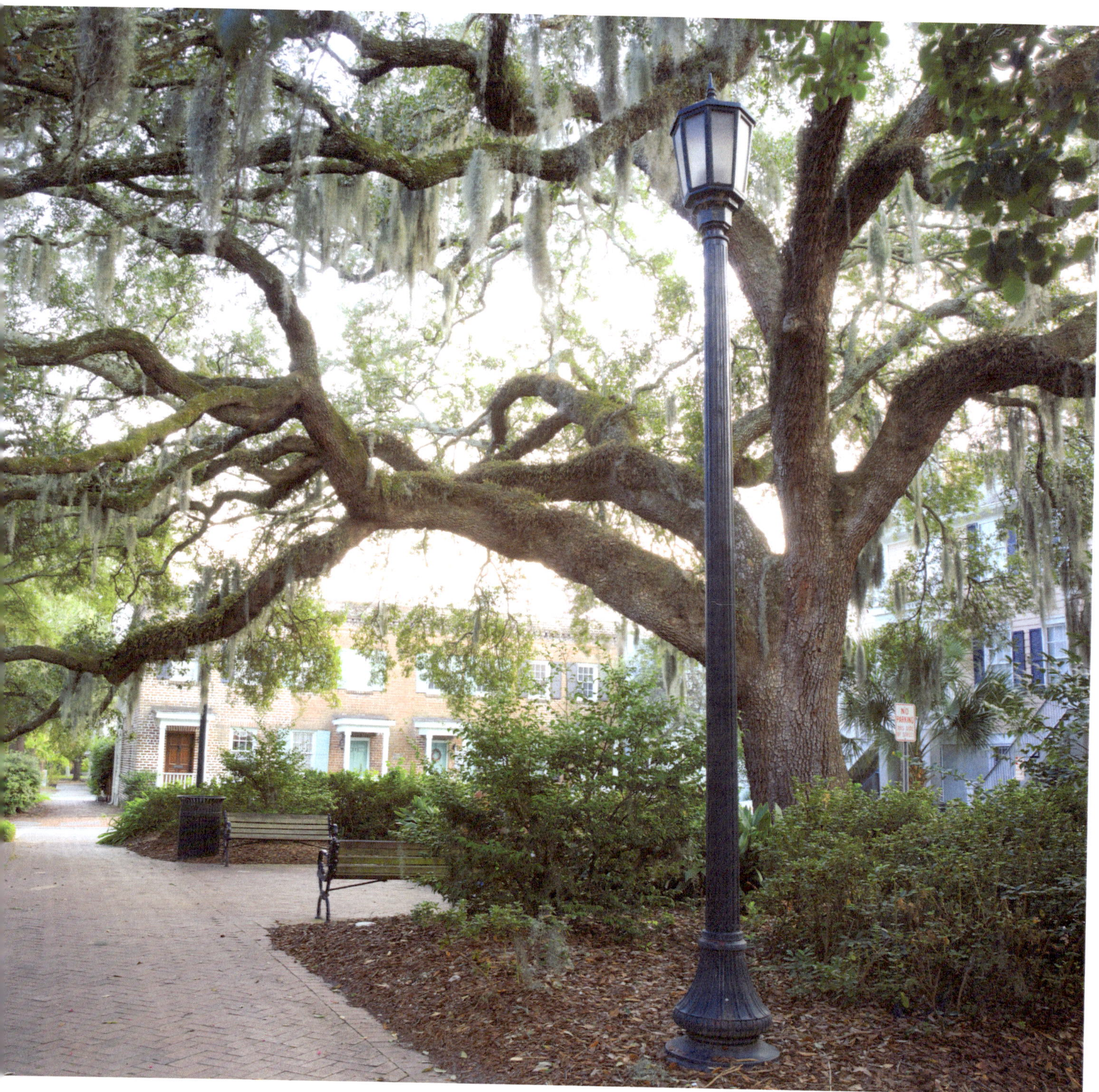

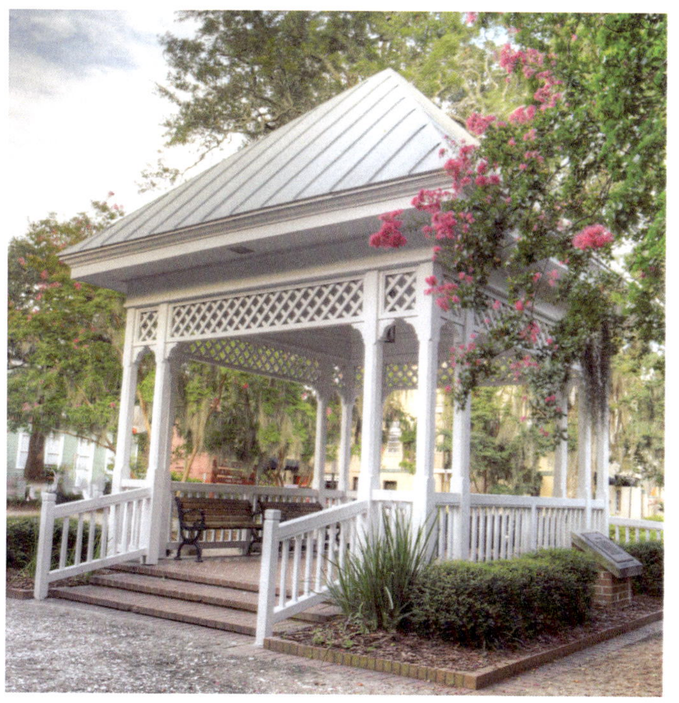

An antique city built on a grid,
Square upon square aligns the small town.
A playground that beckons one's inner kid,
No matter your shape, the options abound.

Cover your eyes and pledge not to peek,
I will then find a prime place to hide,
We'll play a great game of square hide and seek,
In order to win, for you I'll abide.

And then we might meet
In shadows unseen,
And your face I will greet
As we laugh at the scene.

Such games of our youth can establish the day,
You might find yourself each time you play.

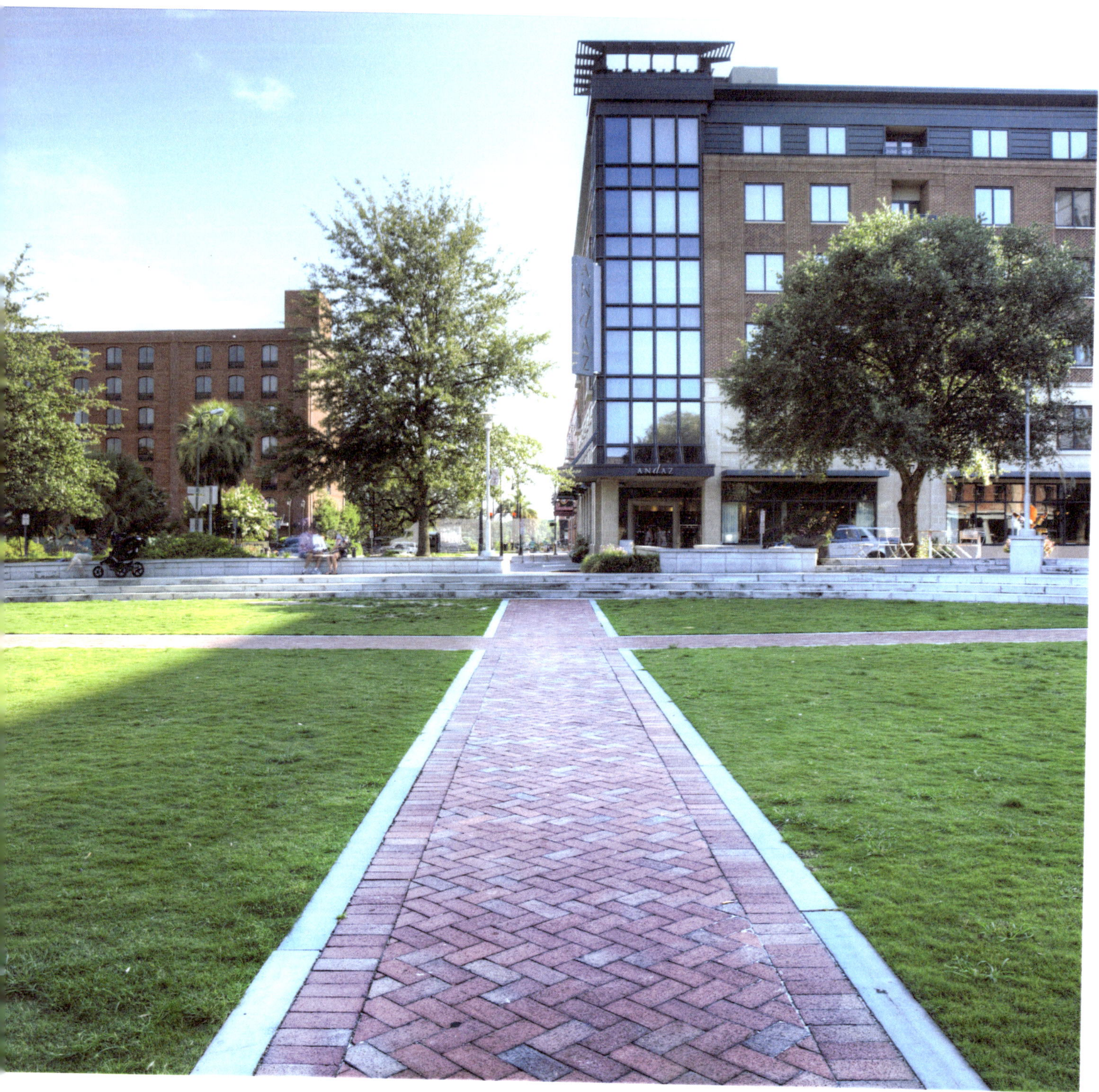

ANDAZ

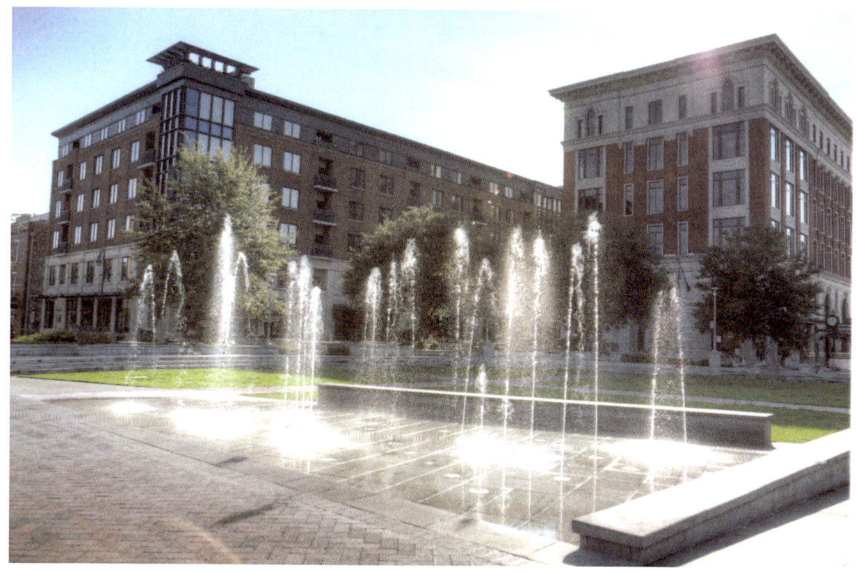

A picturesque walk on a summertime day,
Heavy air flows through ancient trees,
Dogs sniffing, birds chirping, children at play,
An unvoiced respite from the heat in the breeze.

With every small step there is a new sight,
And things left unsaid in a journey through squares,
Beauteous in day and haunting at night,
Present and past both covered and bare.

Treading the cobblestones under your feet,
Bowing to moss draped over your head,
One never knows who by chance you may meet,
In this town of the living and the dead.

Of all the loci to learn of and do,
This Hostess City aims to be true.

Franklin Square

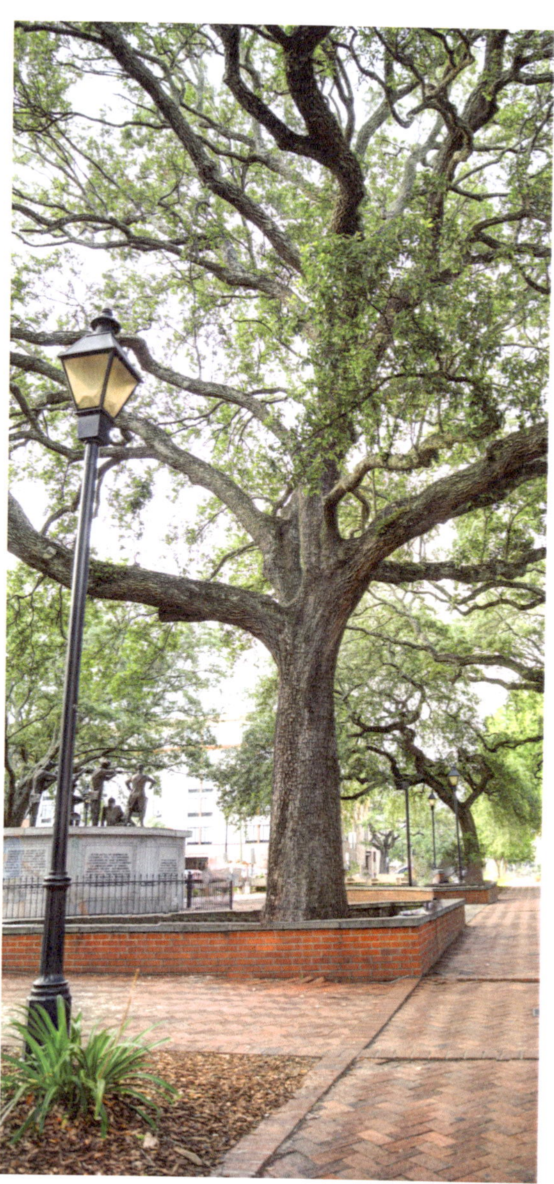

The stories to tell are centuries old,
In buildings of brick and wood and in stone,
The secrets they hold may be foolish or gold,
Walk softly to eavesdrop when you're alone.

The voice of the past resides in the now,
It roams through the stillness found in each square,
Whispering details of who, when, and how,
The fabric and frame of time is laid bare.

We be the ghosts to all future visitors,
We are the secrets this city will keep,
We the attractions of hereafter tours,
We are the dreams when this city does sleep.

Planned by design to align round the square,
Built on a bluff to be open and fair.

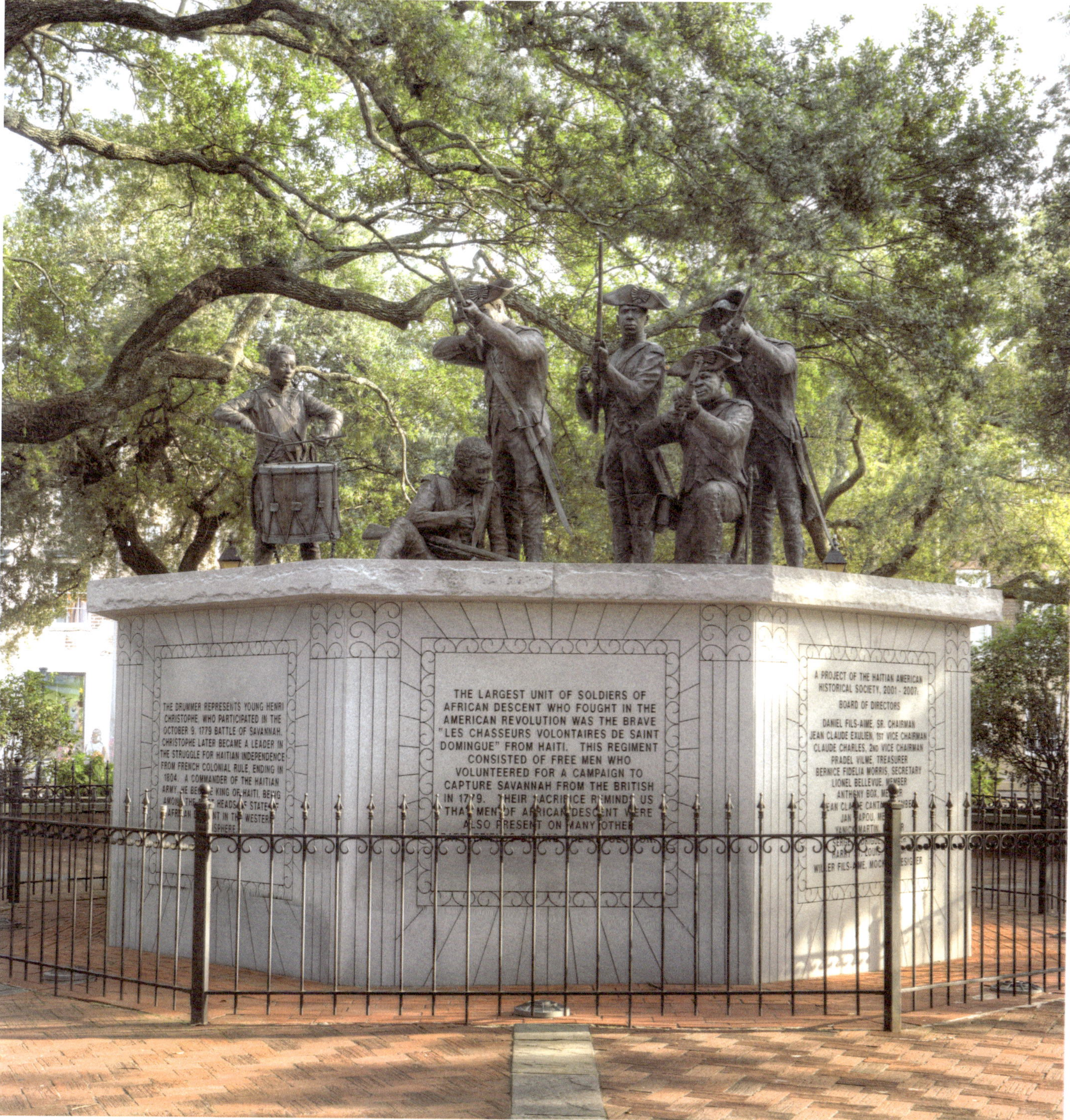

THE DRUMMER REPRESENTS YOUNG HENRI CHRISTOPHE, WHO PARTICIPATED IN THE OCTOBER 9, 1779 BATTLE OF SAVANNAH. CHRISTOPHE LATER BECAME A LEADER IN THE STRUGGLE FOR HAITIAN INDEPENDENCE FROM FRENCH COLONIAL RULE, ENDING IN 1804. A COMMANDER OF THE HAITIAN ARMY, HE BECAME KING OF HAITI, BEING AMONG THE FIRST HEADS OF STATE OF AFRICAN DESCENT IN THE WESTERN HEMISPHERE.

THE LARGEST UNIT OF SOLDIERS OF AFRICAN DESCENT WHO FOUGHT IN THE AMERICAN REVOLUTION WAS THE BRAVE "LES CHASSEURS VOLONTAIRES DE SAINT DOMINGUE" FROM HAITI. THIS REGIMENT CONSISTED OF FREE MEN WHO VOLUNTEERED FOR A CAMPAIGN TO CAPTURE SAVANNAH FROM THE BRITISH IN 1779. THEIR SACRIFICE REMINDS US THAT MEN OF AFRICAN DESCENT WERE ALSO PRESENT ON MANY OTHER

A PROJECT OF THE HAITIAN AMERICAN HISTORICAL SOCIETY, 2001 - 2007.
BOARD OF DIRECTORS
DANIEL FILS-AIME, SR. CHAIRMAN
JEAN CLAUDE EXULIEN, 1st VICE CHAIRMAN
CLAUDE CHARLES, 2nd VICE CHAIRMAN
PRADEL VILME, TREASURER
BERNICE FIDELIA MORRIS, SECRETARY
LIONEL BELLEVUE, MEMBER
ANTHONY BOX, MEMBER
JEAN CLAUDE CANTAVE, MEMBER
JAN MAPOU, MEMBER
YANICK MARTIN, MEMBER
HARRY ST. LOUIS
WILLER FILS-AIME, MOCK DESIGNER

Greene Square

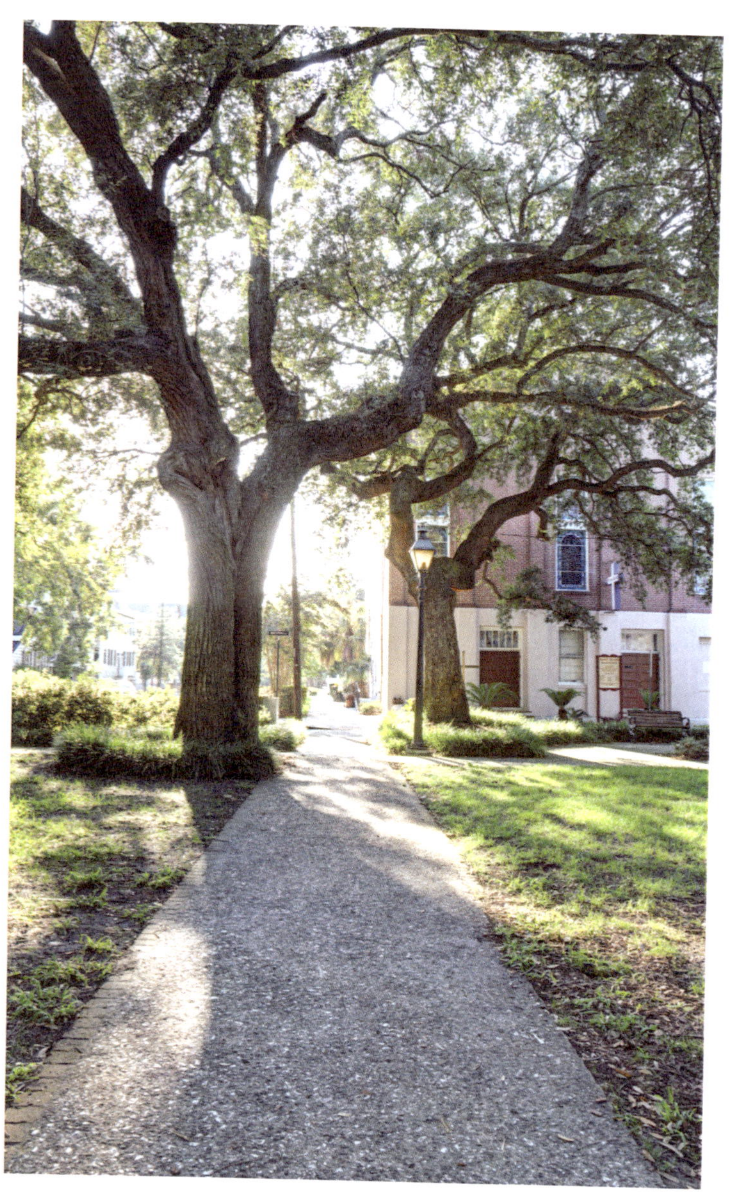

An artist paints what an artist can see,
Whether it is with the eyes or the mind,
Unlock your sight and the artist is free,
There is no end to the beauty you'll find.

The knots of a tree, the veins of a leaf,
The shadows between each blade of grass,
From sounds of joy to tears of grief,
Observing the world as eternities pass.

The painter's canvas stretches so vast,
All of creation within this one frame,
The future blends through the brush of the past,
Each is an artist regardless of fame.

Paint boldly and often and from the heart,
Our lives are what make the best works of art.

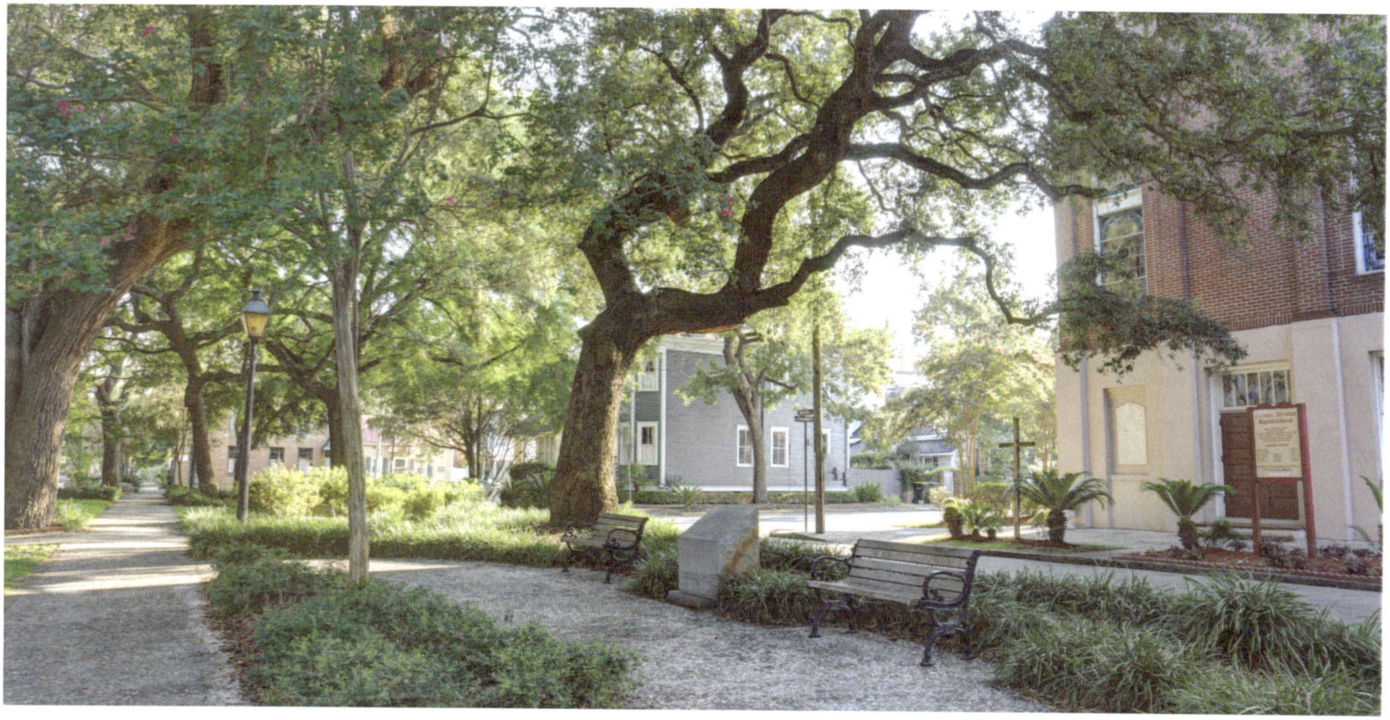

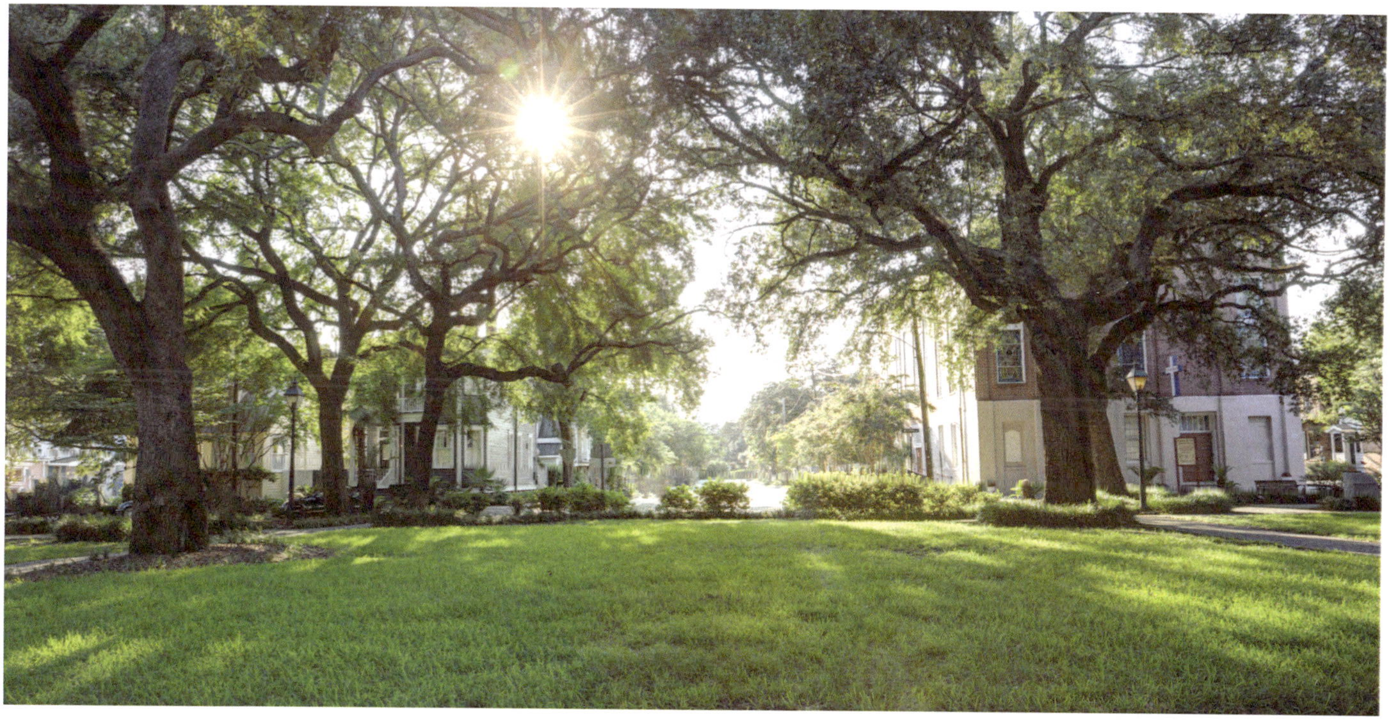

Johnson Square

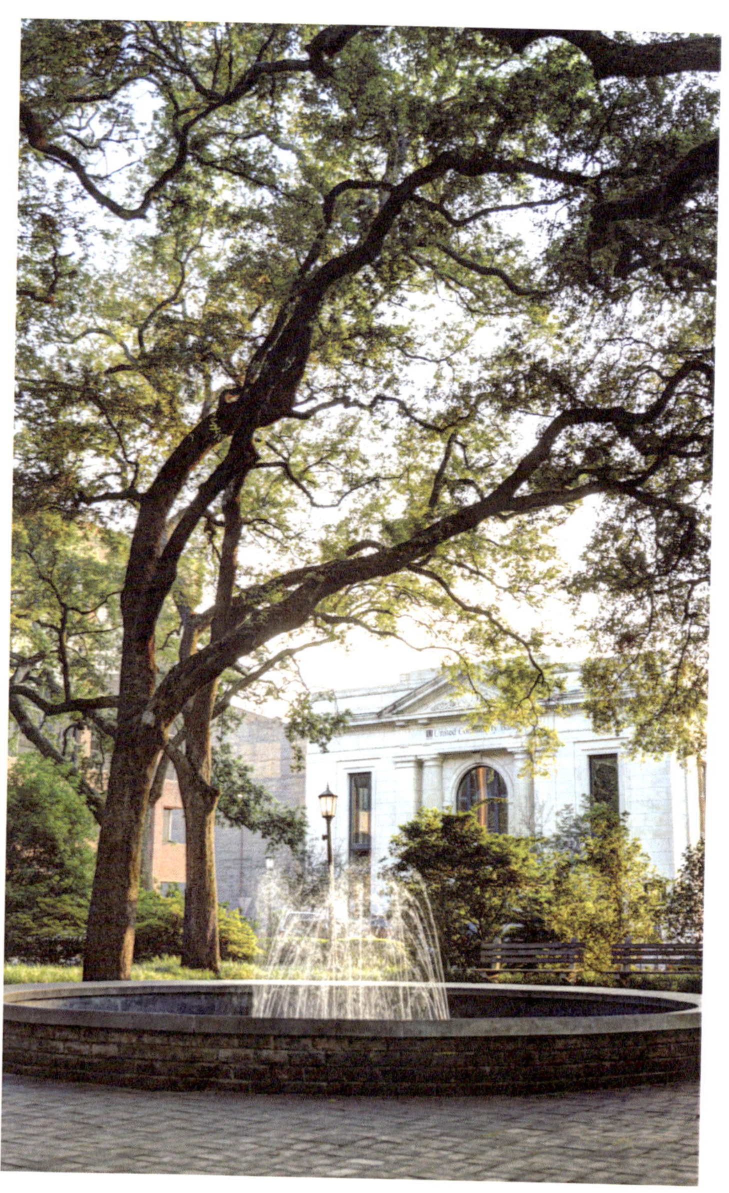

Memories are tools for traveling time,
Reality's borders are willowy and weak;
One's mind can behold unraveling time,
Draw back the veil and take just a peek.

The journey is short to most yesterdays,
Old places familiar we easily haunt,
Our thoughts and our hopes peel past away,
Go there to visit whenever we want.

This knowledge assured we must ensure to act,
Weaving each moment aware it will last,
All will endure in some shape or fact,
There isn't a future, there isn't a past.

A flawless moment in an unblemished place,
Can shine like a ruby across time and space.

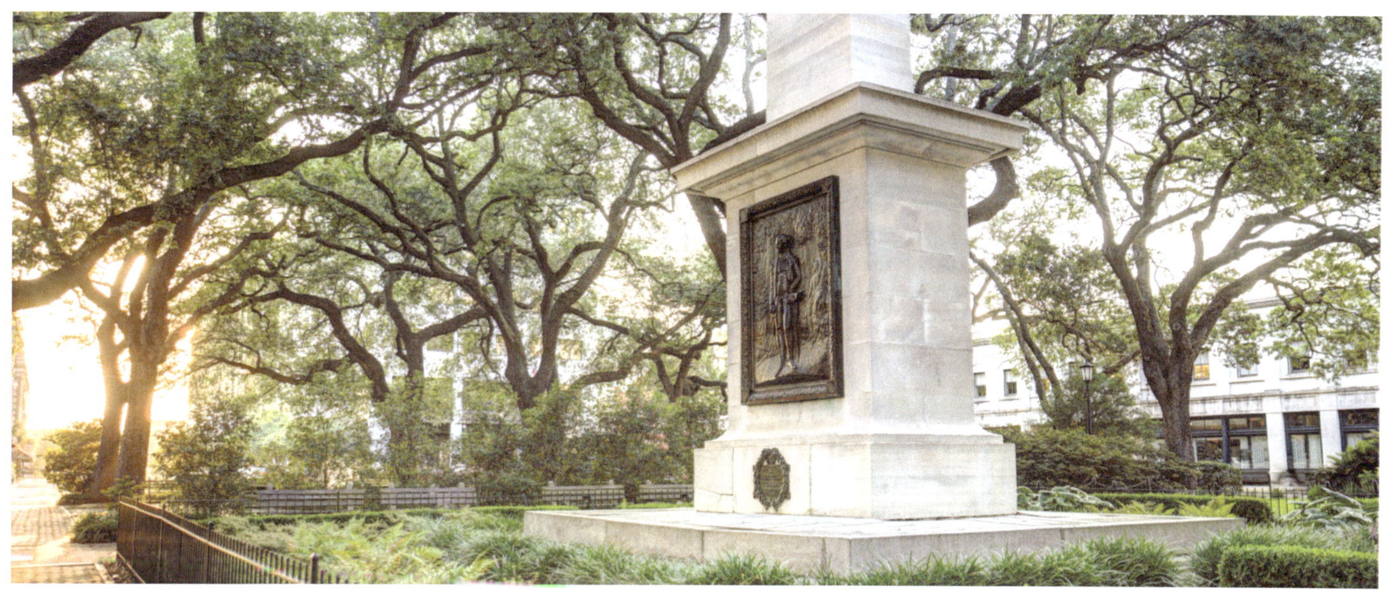

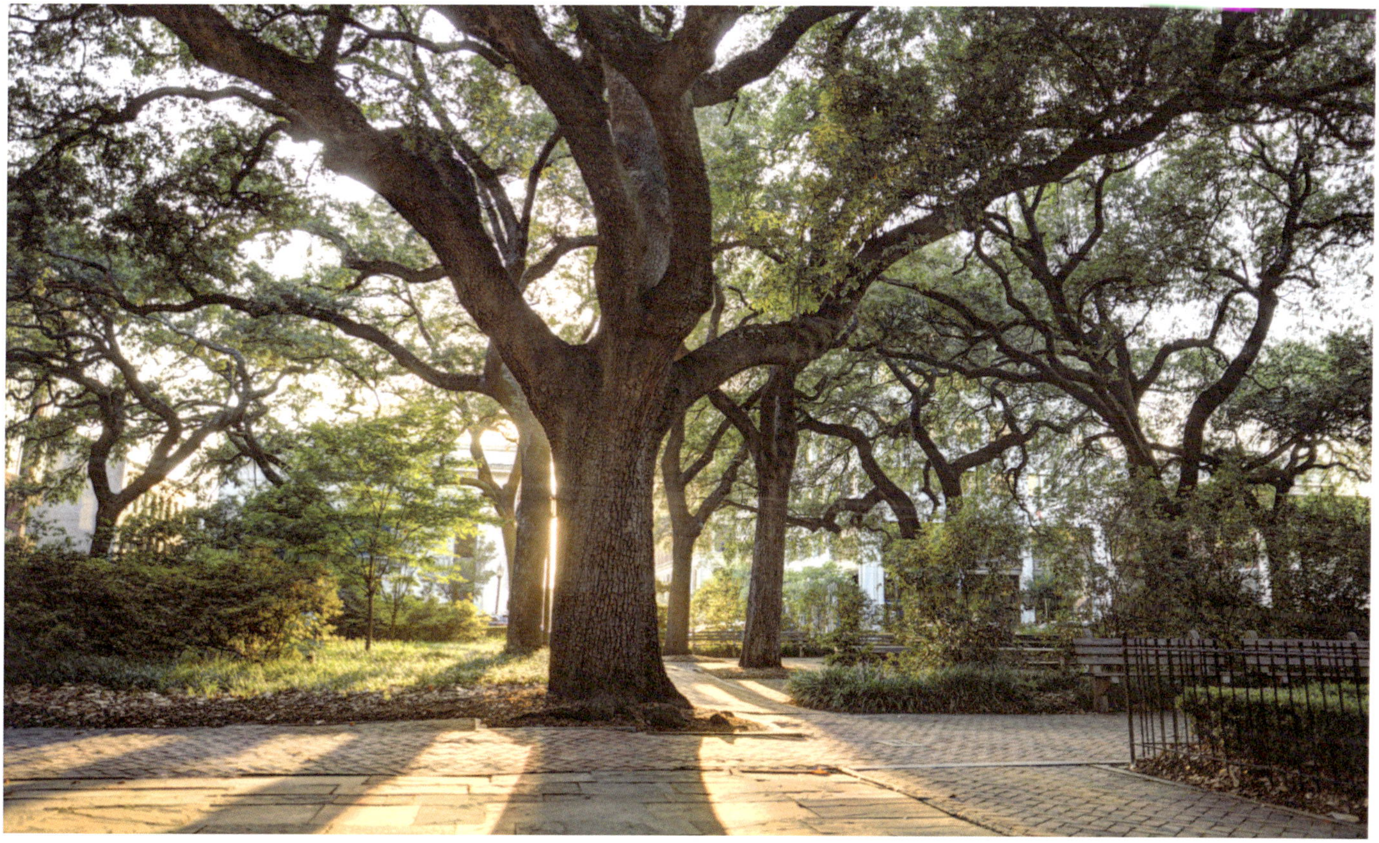

Lafayette Square

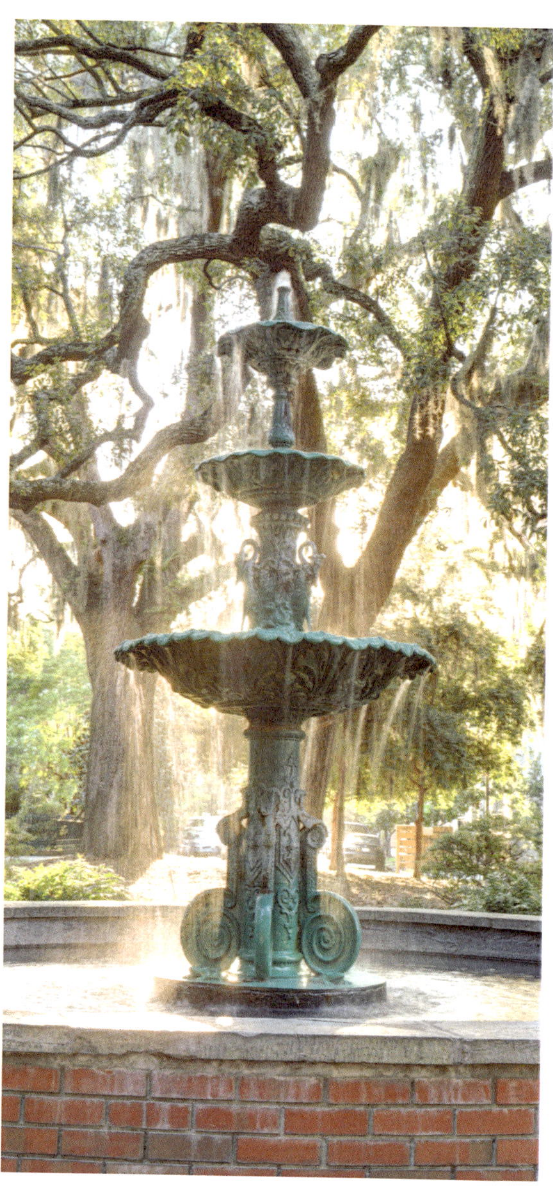

The winter cold pales, but not the summer heat,
Spring eternally awaits to appear,
A gentle fall is all that is sweet:
A seasonal dance is this city's souvenir.

Summer, of course, takes the passionate lead,
Autumn then follows with a sensual flair.
Winter cuts in, somewhat solemn and freed,
But in jetés spring with great leaps through the air.

So many will watch the parade passing by,
Month after month how the seasons will dance,
Regardless of music, you just need to try,
A tango, a two-step, a modern-day prance.

Rhythm and time form the seasons of life,
Rooted in sounds of the drum and the fife.

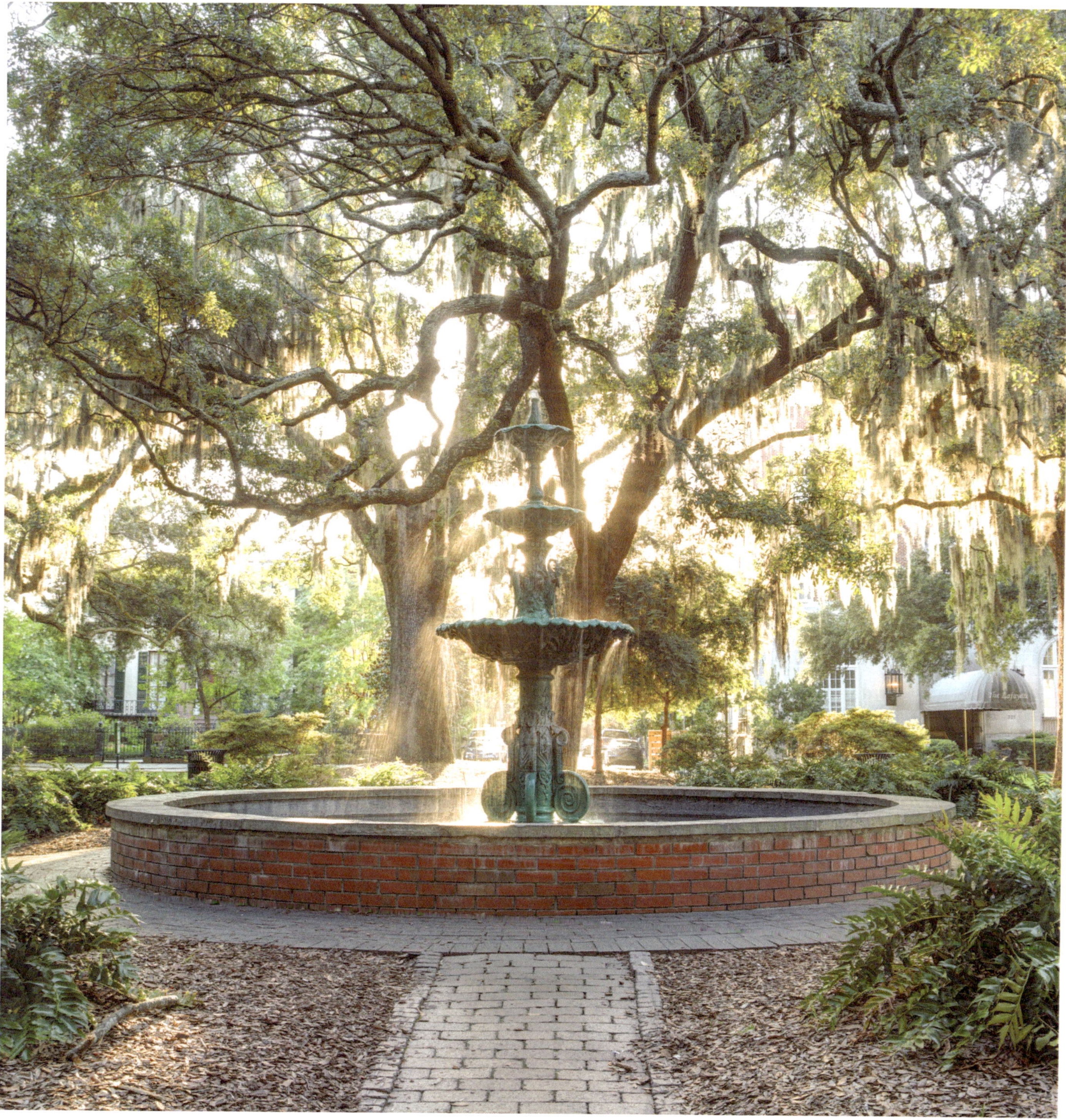

Maneuver the squares — to the left or the right?
The historical plan but a chessboard.
But not for a king or a queen or a knight,
Or even milady or milord.

Yet the great game's afoot, and one plays to win,
Square by square you traverse through the town,
Get a dirty martini with ethereal gin,
Or a meat and three to chow down.

All are welcome to play in this grand checkered game,
And experience the joys and the strife,
Those who win will find more than fortune and fame,
It is a wonderful game we call life.

However you move just come out and play,
The odds will be smiling both night and day.

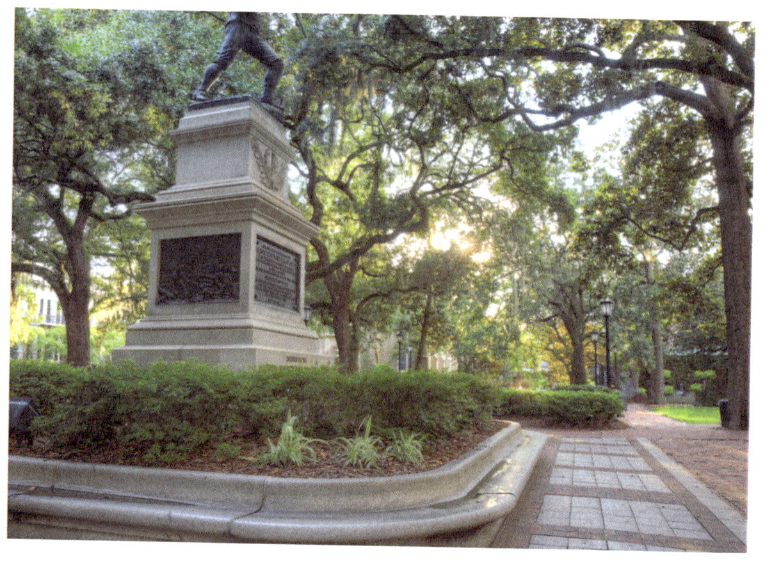

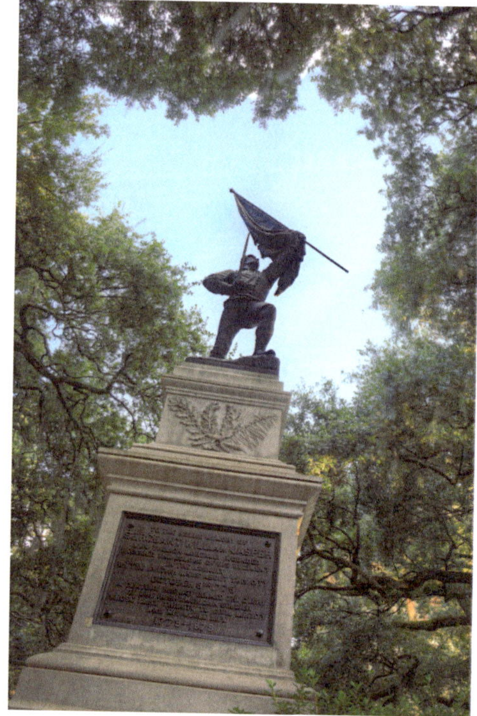

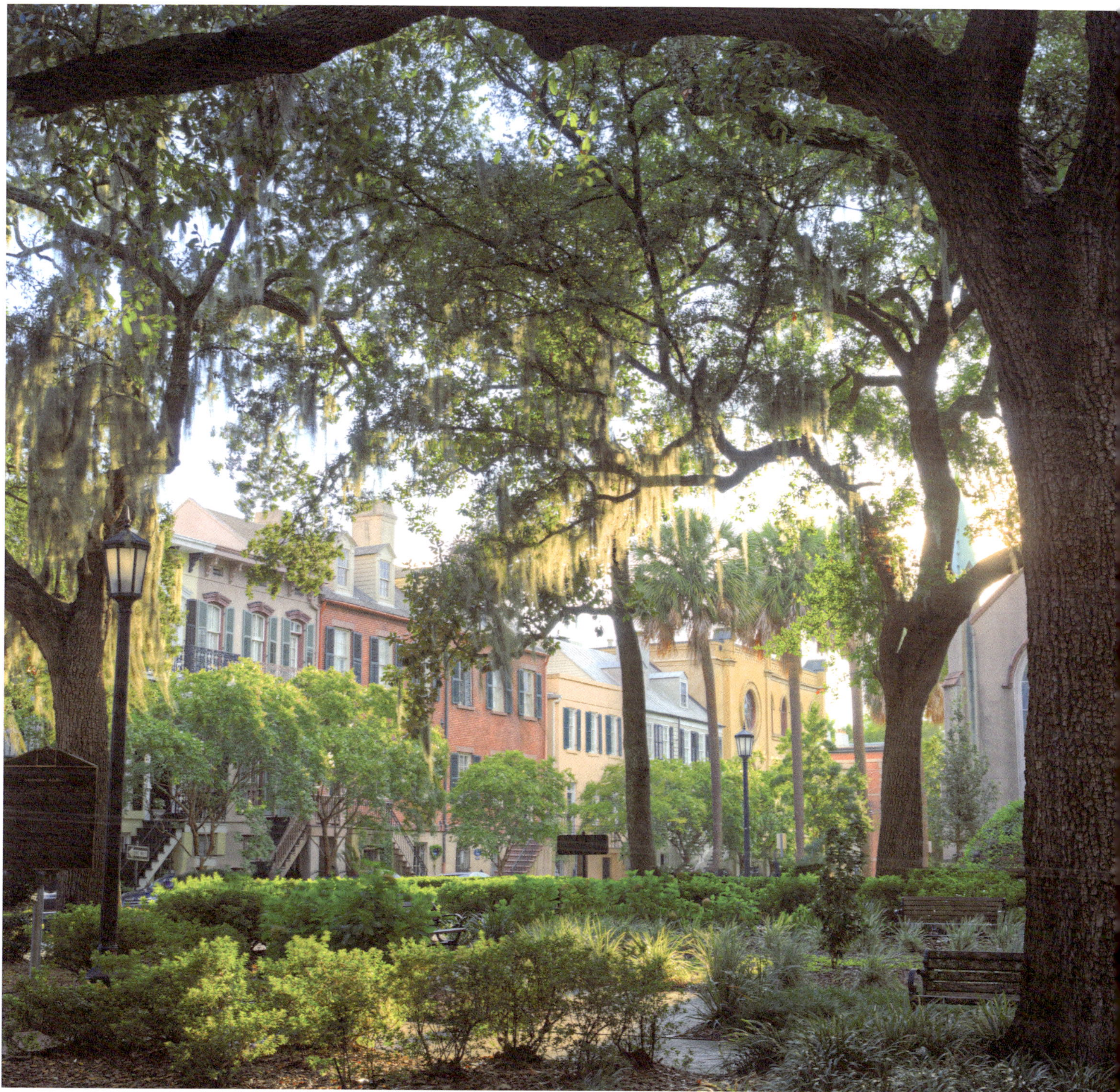

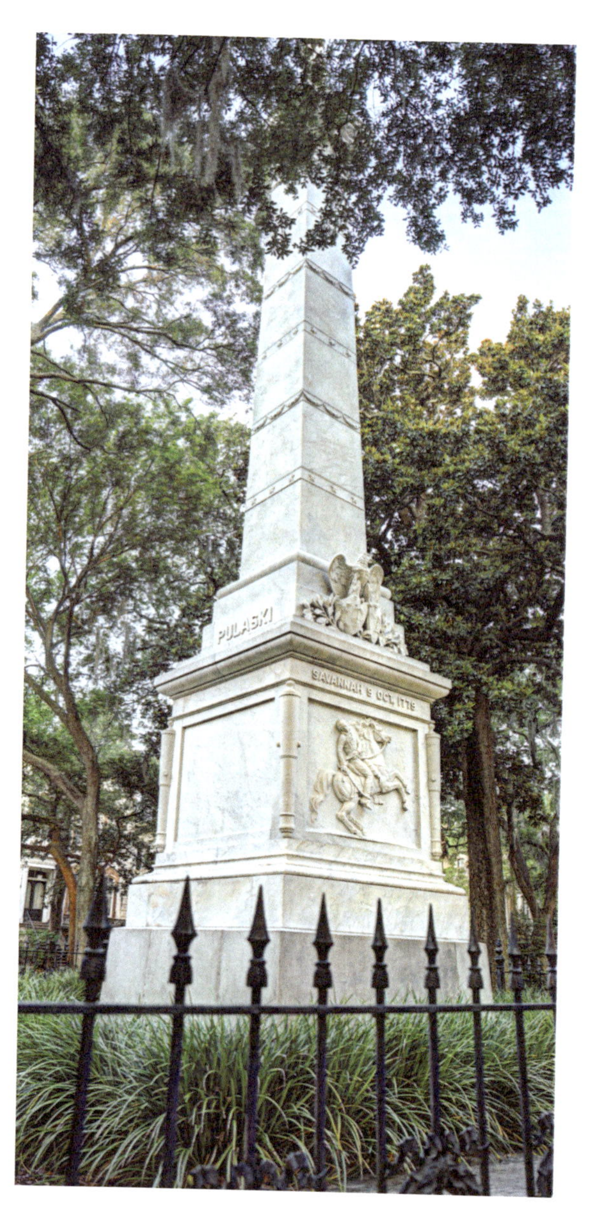

A small city in the southern states,
Wherein mystery, romance, and more awaits:
Lost souls, some found, and tangled fates,
Old battles, hidden histories, and foregone dates.

On the shore of dreams the real world abates,
And one stands aright at fantasy's gates
Where past and present are perfect mates,
Drawn together by their parallel traits.

With loves long lost and deep buried hates,
And wells of sorrow that both create,
The times of hunger that cannot sate,
The descending starkness to which all relate.

We are served our lives on silver plates,
And share table together with the greats.

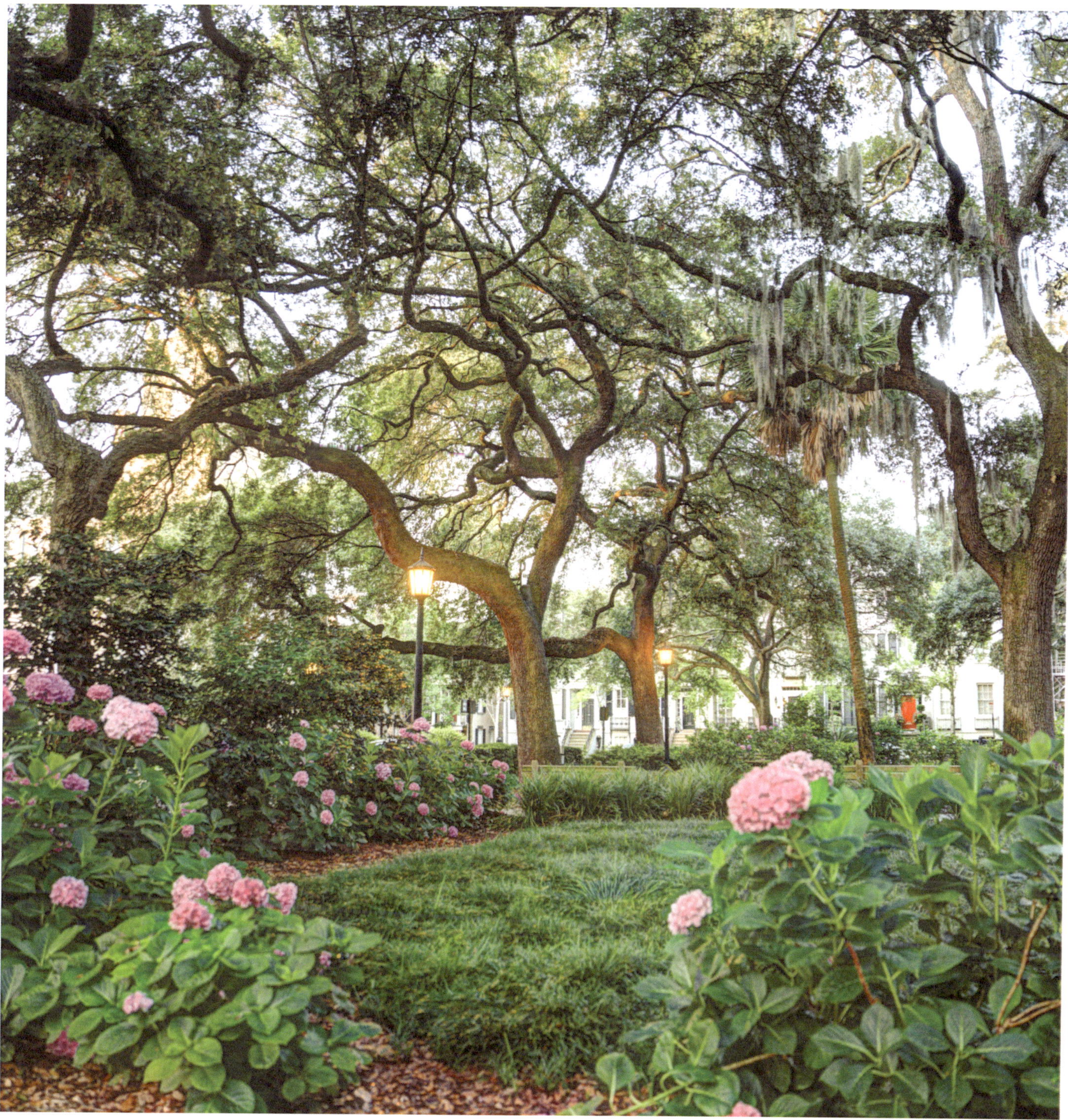

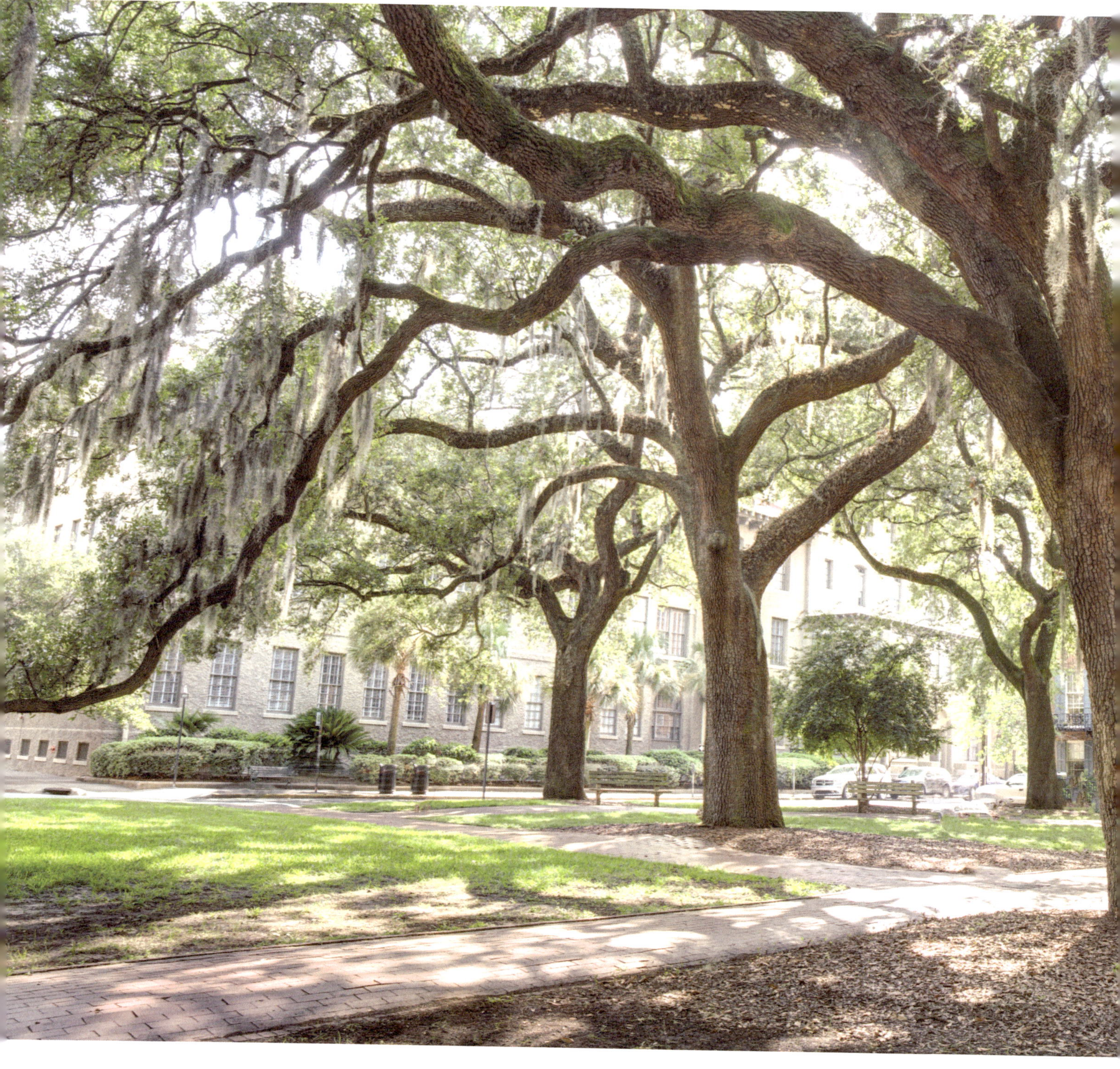

Oglethorpe Square

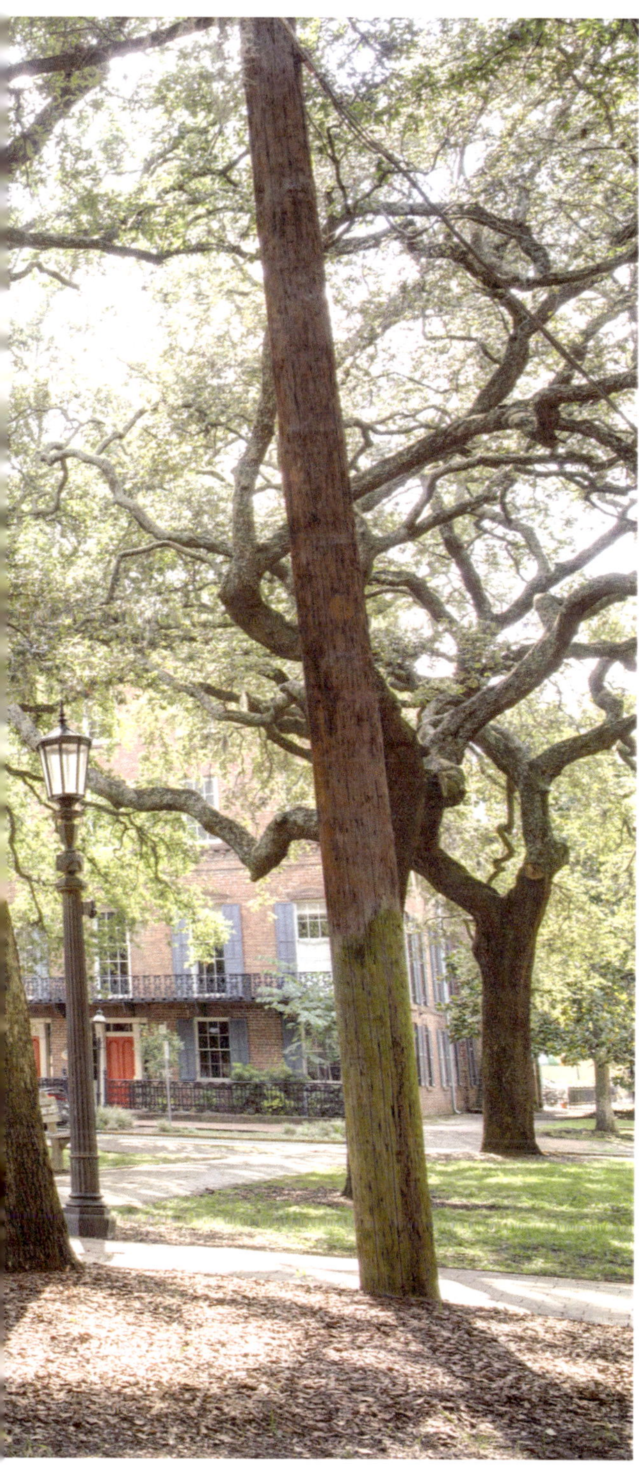

Place plays a part when we trip into love
Or seek out a scene as a mood strikes,
Grass 'neath your feet, tree branches above,
As we rest or we stroll or even ride bikes.

An atmosphere sparks an air of romance,
The places, O places, that tug at your heart,
Become a new partner in our worldly dance,
Surrounded we are by this great work of art.

There are places we hold, both the near and the dear,
There are places we know where magic doth live,
We weave our memories, both faded and clear,
We take and we take yet the city still gives.

Home is where the heart settles, 'tis true,
But home is also where love will find you.

Rest and retreat in each day that's given,
Carve out the time to breathe in fresh air;
Savor the sun and for what it has striven,
Turn inward to see what the mind's eye will lay bare.

Hard days are those filled with striving and strife
And do not define the essence of you;
Let not worries and wrangles rule over your life
But the myriad things that you choose to do.

A ramble through nature, an eavesdrop of birds,
Far from the imitative world where we work,
Summon the silence away from all words,
Break from the places where stresses do lurk.

Our magnum opus is a life of peace,
A master artwork where all weights cease.

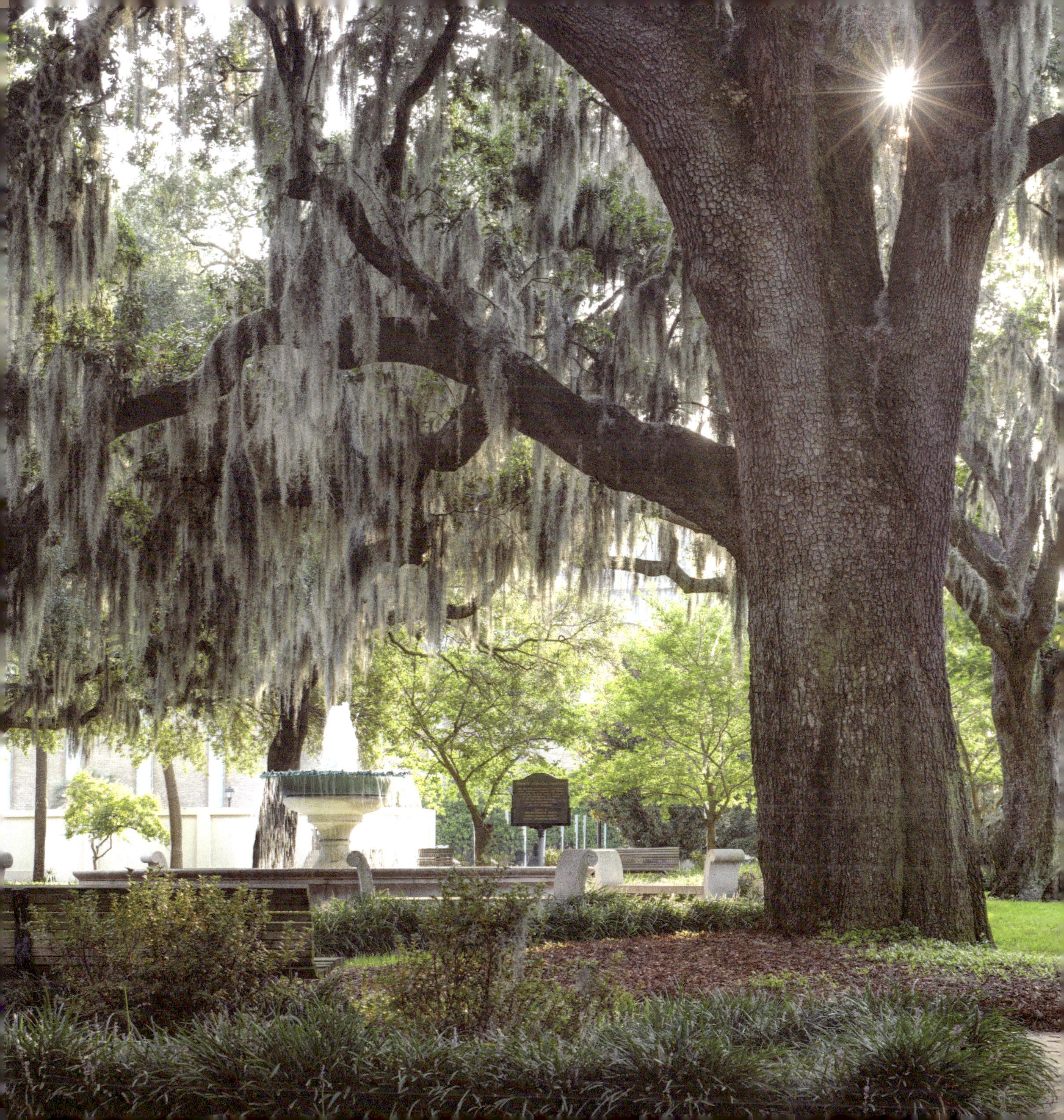

Pulaski Square

The hanging moss start a pendent dance
To silent music only they seem to hear;
Swaying softly, so softly, as if in a trance,
Swaying wayfarers beneath them with wonder and cheer.

The melody carries to all points in the square,
Delighting those traversing the pathway;
All who visit or pass secretly know that it's there,
This tune that plays on night and day.

If e'er you seek a stroll through a park,
Don't listen with ears but attend with the heart;
The music so soundless will leave a clear mark,
Though the harmony obliges that you play a part.

The magical movements that structure this symphony
Sounds you can't hear and sights you can't see.

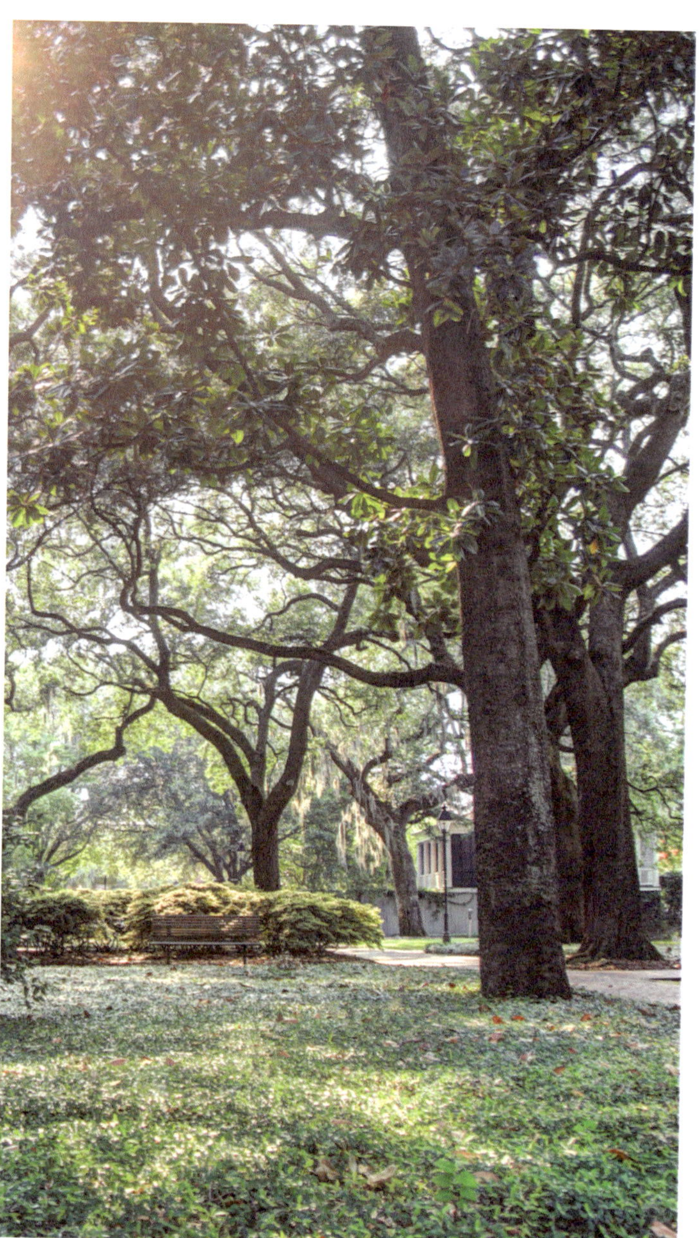

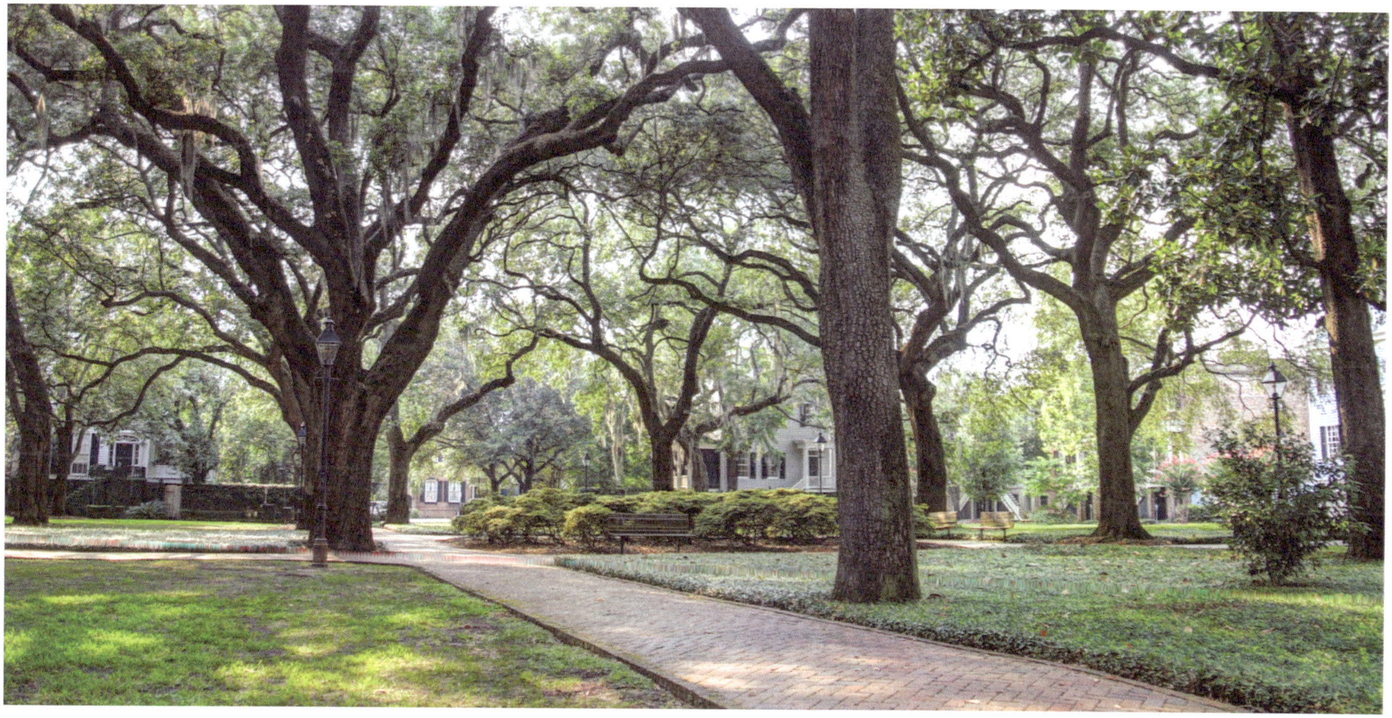

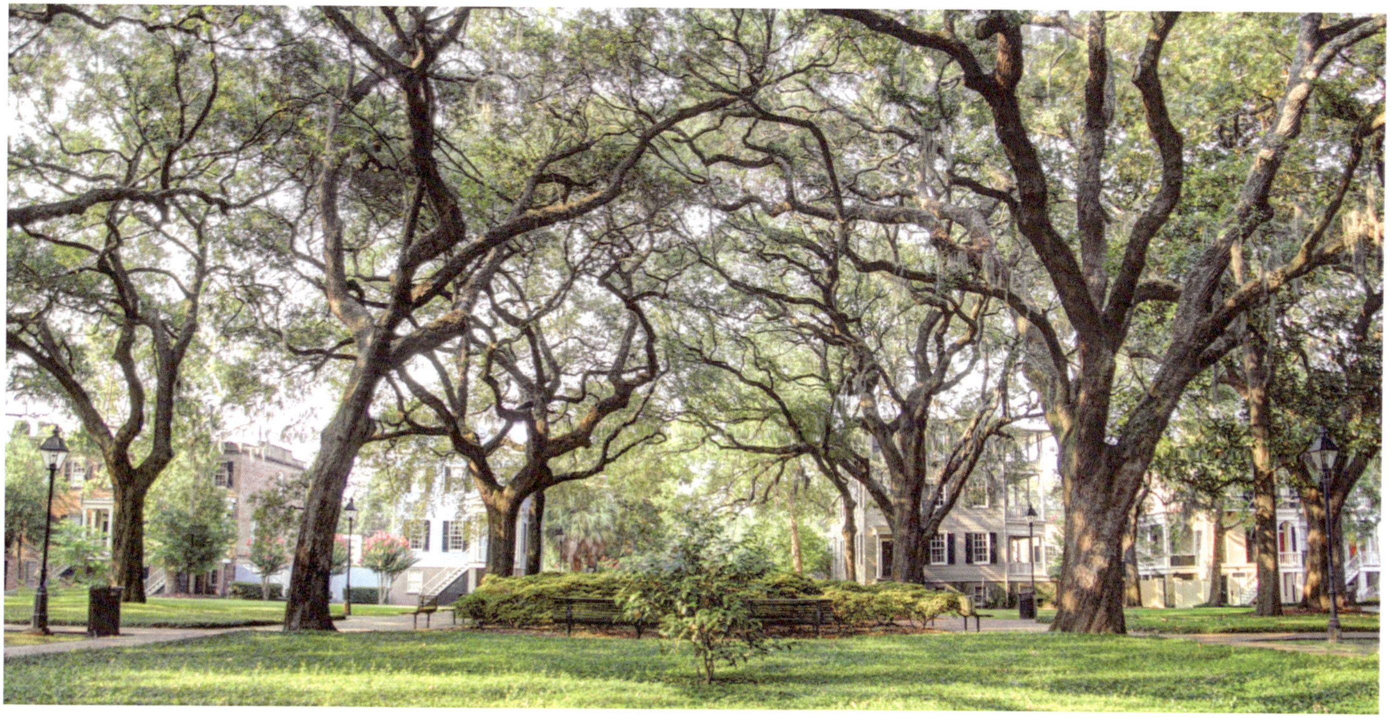

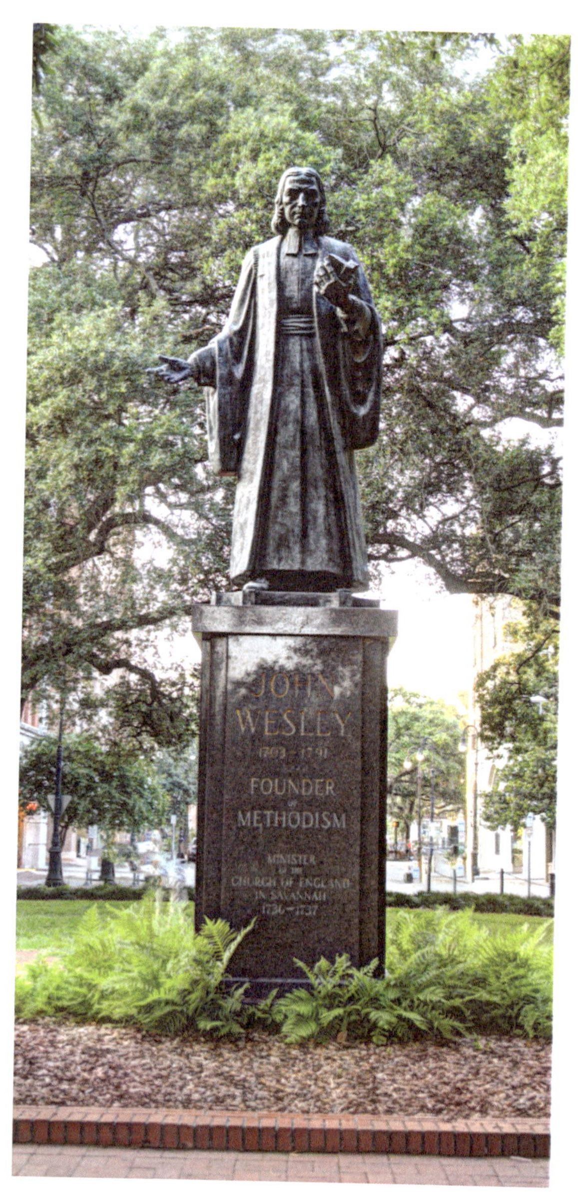

Eyes closed I lift my face to the sun,
The light finds its way through my eyelids.
Then when I blink the light is not done,
A ghost star now beckons and bids.

Follow the phantom through the green square,
Bouncing off bench and from tree to tree,
What wonderful treasures will I find there?
I feel that the city belongs now to me.

The checkerboard landscape tempts like a game,
The rules are scant and a perfume infuses.
The city knows me and whispers my name,
I am among the many it chooses.

This city of squares declares I belong,
I gladly abide for it is not wrong.

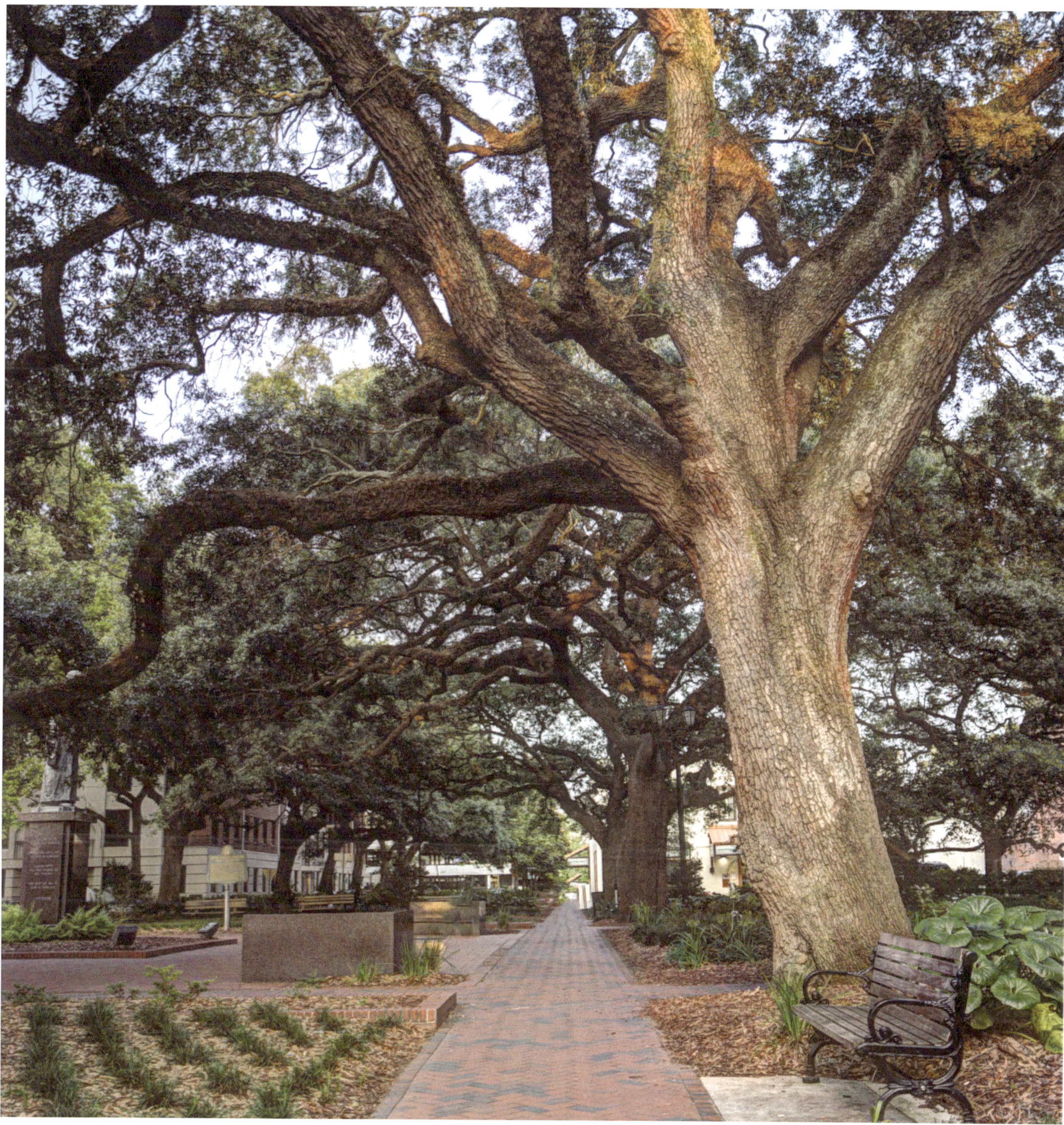

Taylor Square

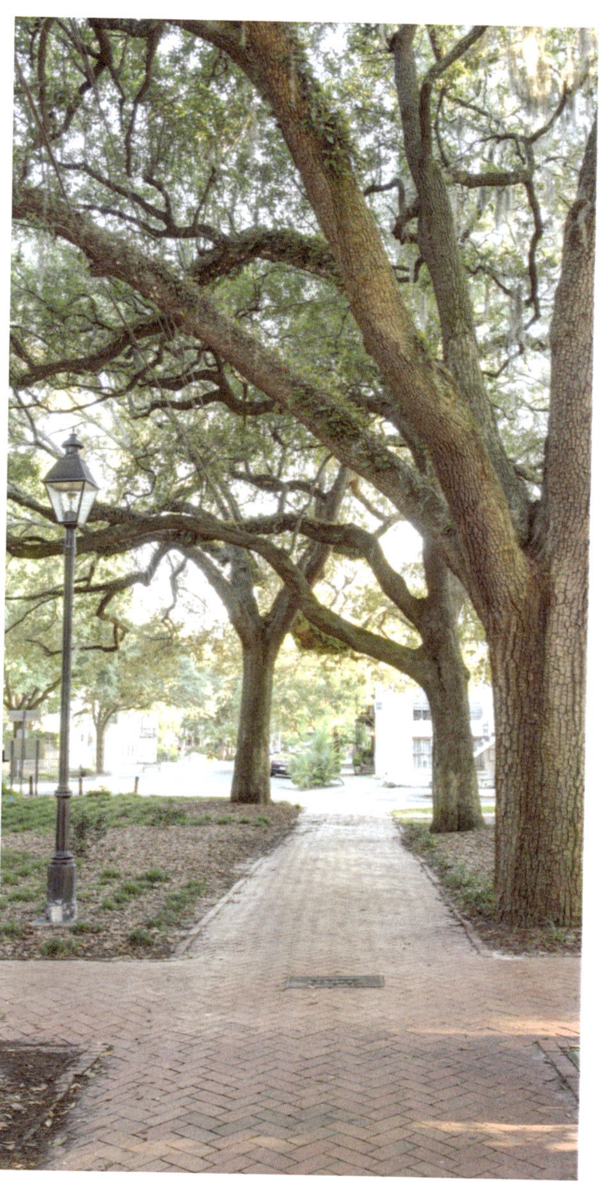

Pigeons fly about searching for a perch,
A statue or monument the fleeting ideal.
At times the winged tourists are left in the lurch,
As certain sculptures lack all appeal.

Some are too wrathful with faces quite mean,
Some are too tragic where sorrows run deep.
Tricky to find a haunt in between,
A joyful place for the pigeons to keep.

One statue depicts a soldier who died,
Another is of a soldier at war;
One monument is for the tears we have cried,
One memorial is for not wanting more.

Life for the birds demands places to nest.
Life for us all is remembering our best.

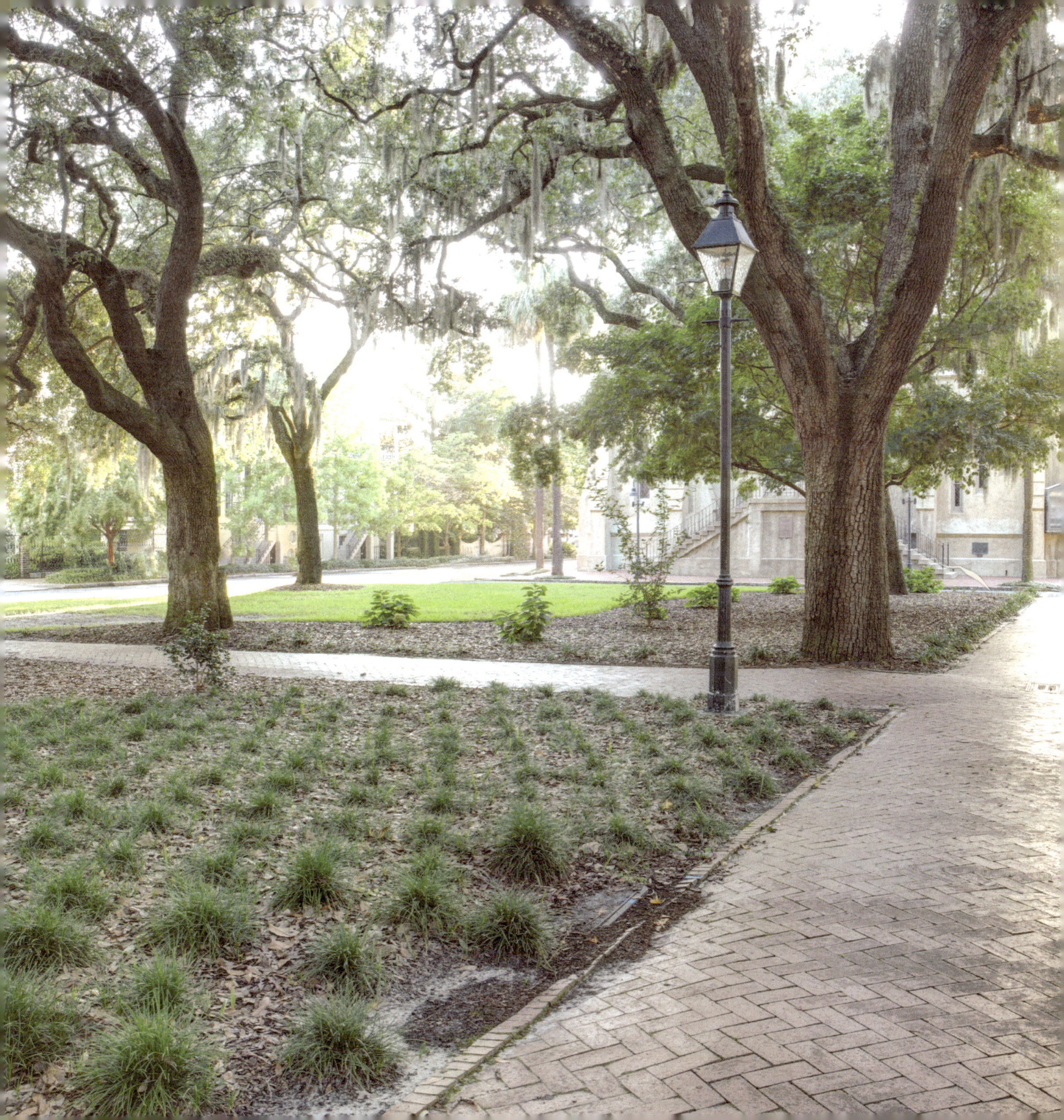

Telfair Square

If e'er the seasons do change for me,
Let them be soft and O so mild,
Allow passage of time to go gently,
Like a spring day in the life of a child.

Let green cling to grass and every oak,
Let sorrow be a sight never we see.
Let woe burn away in the fire it stokes,
Let summer rain sweep away each pain from me.

I can forgive Father Time for his endless trek,
I may be satisfied and sated with all that I know,
If all of history is at my beck,
I can look beyond the coming tomorrow.

The world holds her place, we've been here before,
I revel in her grace and beauty evermore.

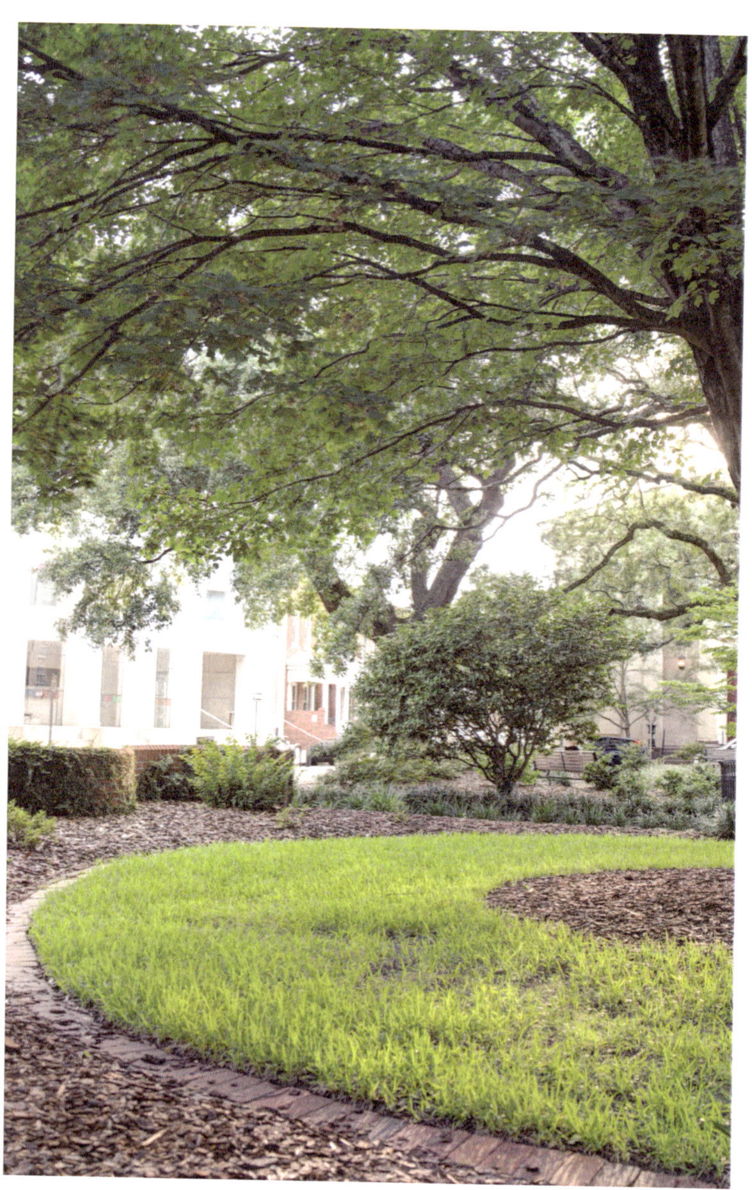

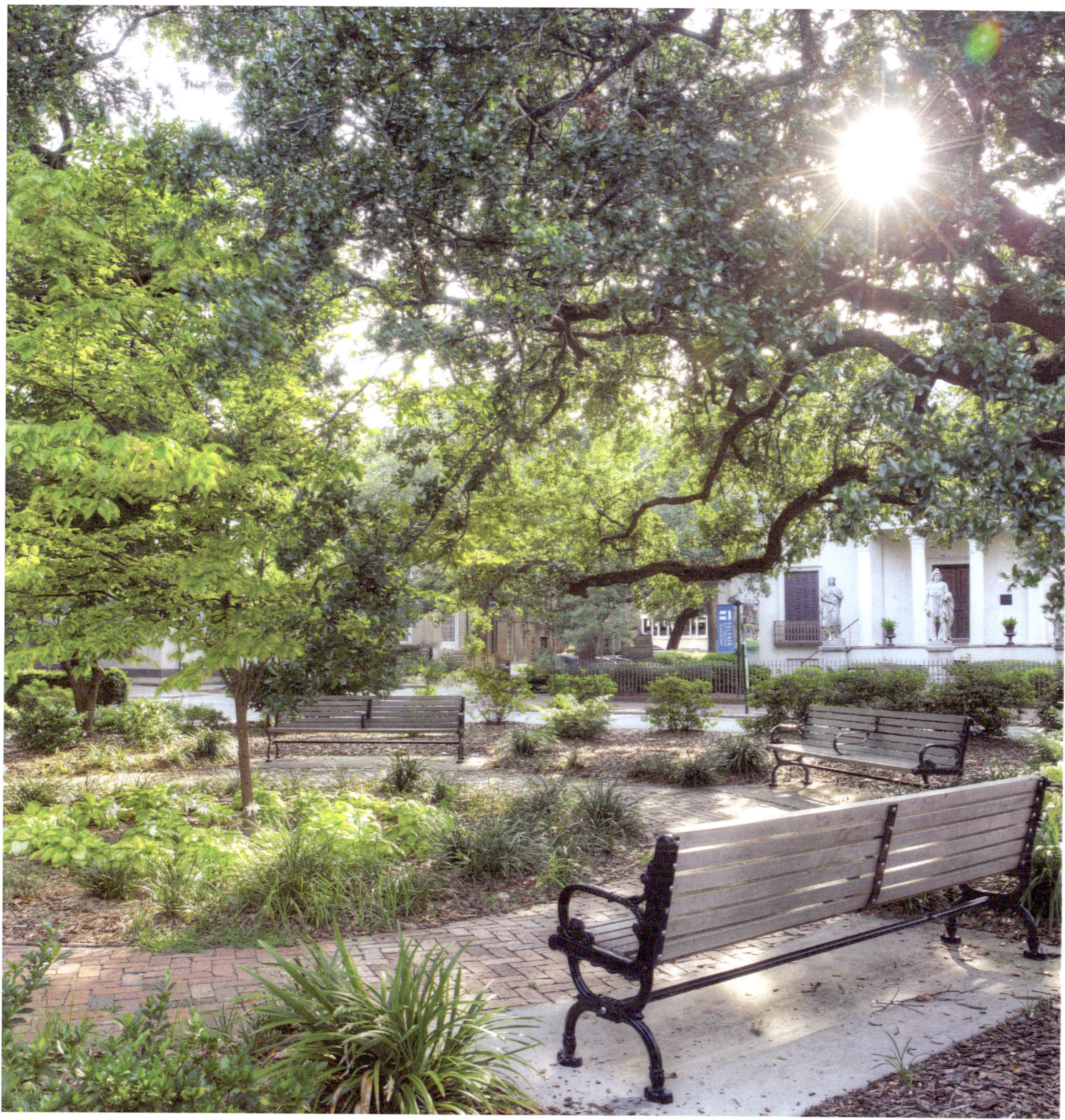

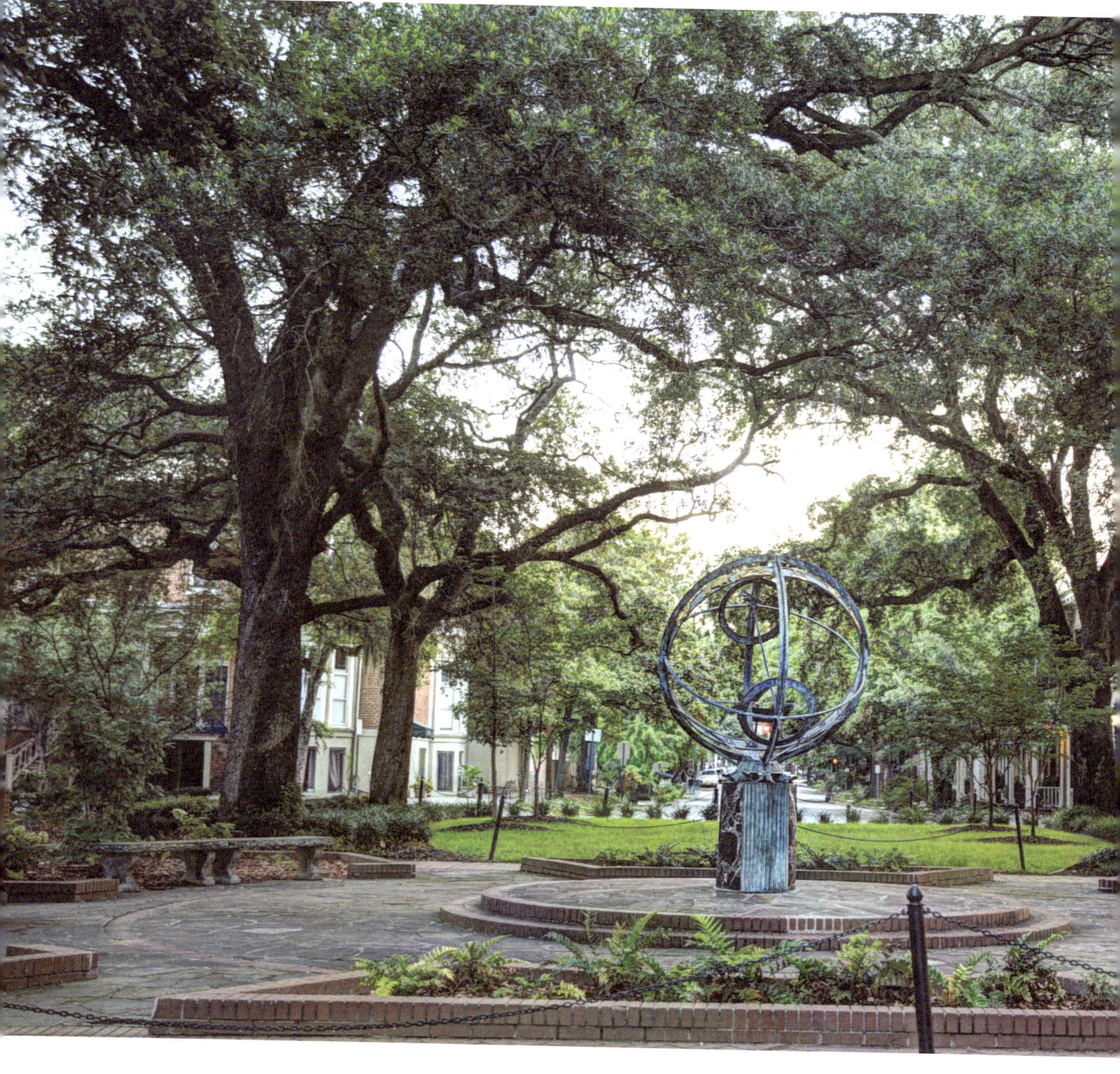

Troup Square

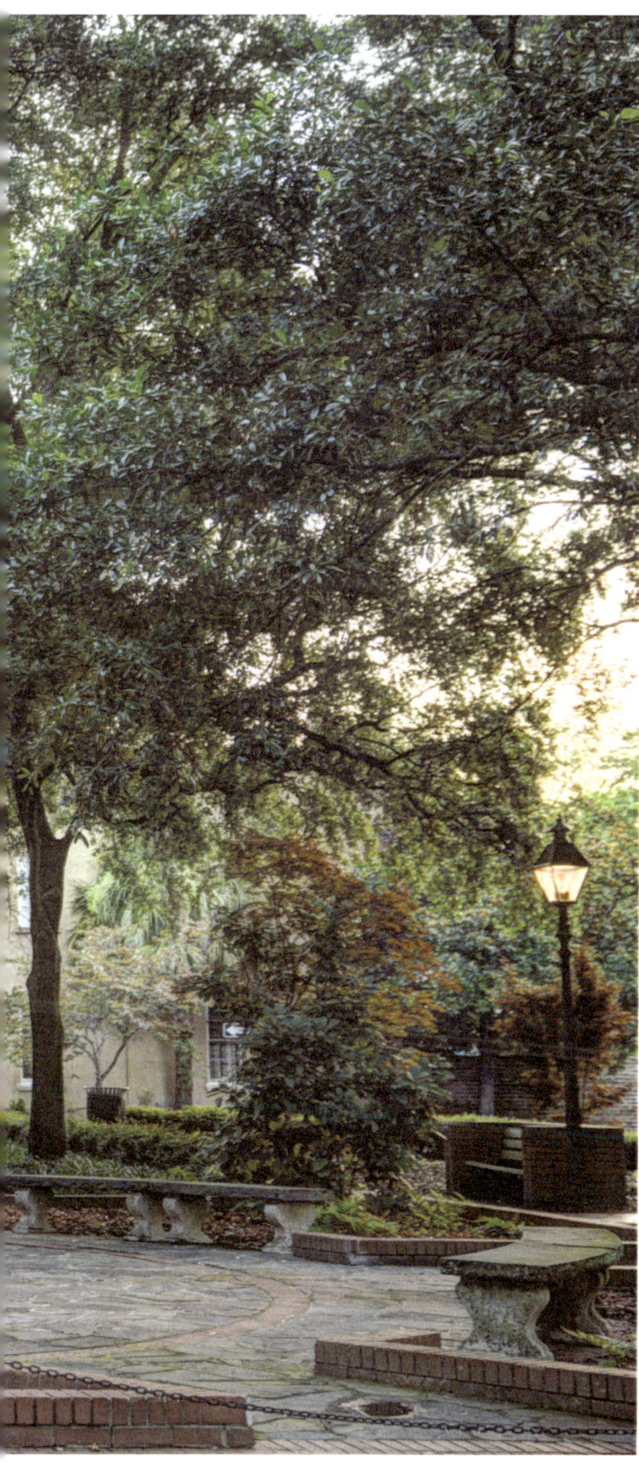

Savannah, O Hostess City of the South!
Behold her hair flowing of silken moss,
Glimpse the knowing smile on her mouth,
Her eyes have seen great joy and greater loss.

She does her best to keep secrets hid,
She blushes with heat on a June day.
She cools at the breath of a winter's bid.
She's noble and silent but has much to say.

She graces the ballroom, sagacious and young,
Dance with her when evening music does play,
Sing along when old songs are asked to be sung,
Loving her is to court both joy and dismay.

Lay under the curtain where stars have been strung,
Do not cross her or wound her or risk being stung.

Warren Square

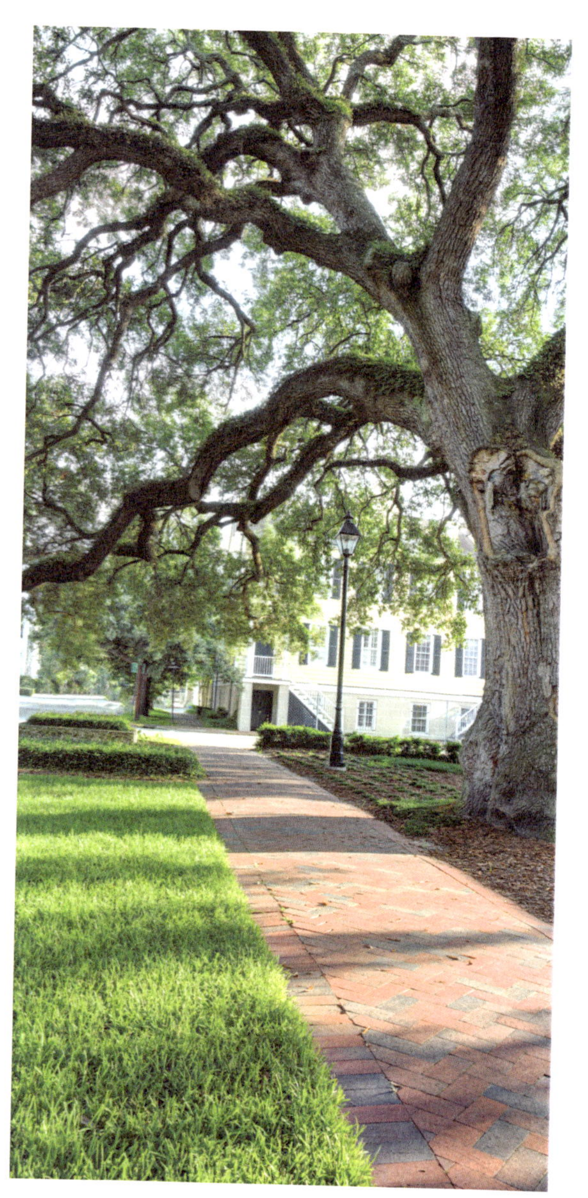

The weighted air with humidity thick,
Subduing those who venture out,
The scorching heat on the skin does stick,
A summer's day is its own redoubt.

But once one spies the wise of the sun,
An escape may be found from the day's heat,
In the shade of trees there may come even fun,
Ice cream (or mixed spirits) will bring a cool treat.

There are those who complain and those who blame,
And those who never depart their house,
But boredom's heat is just the same.
Heed the advice that I espouse:

Encounter adventure and a life come alive,
Do not wait for cool weather to arrive.

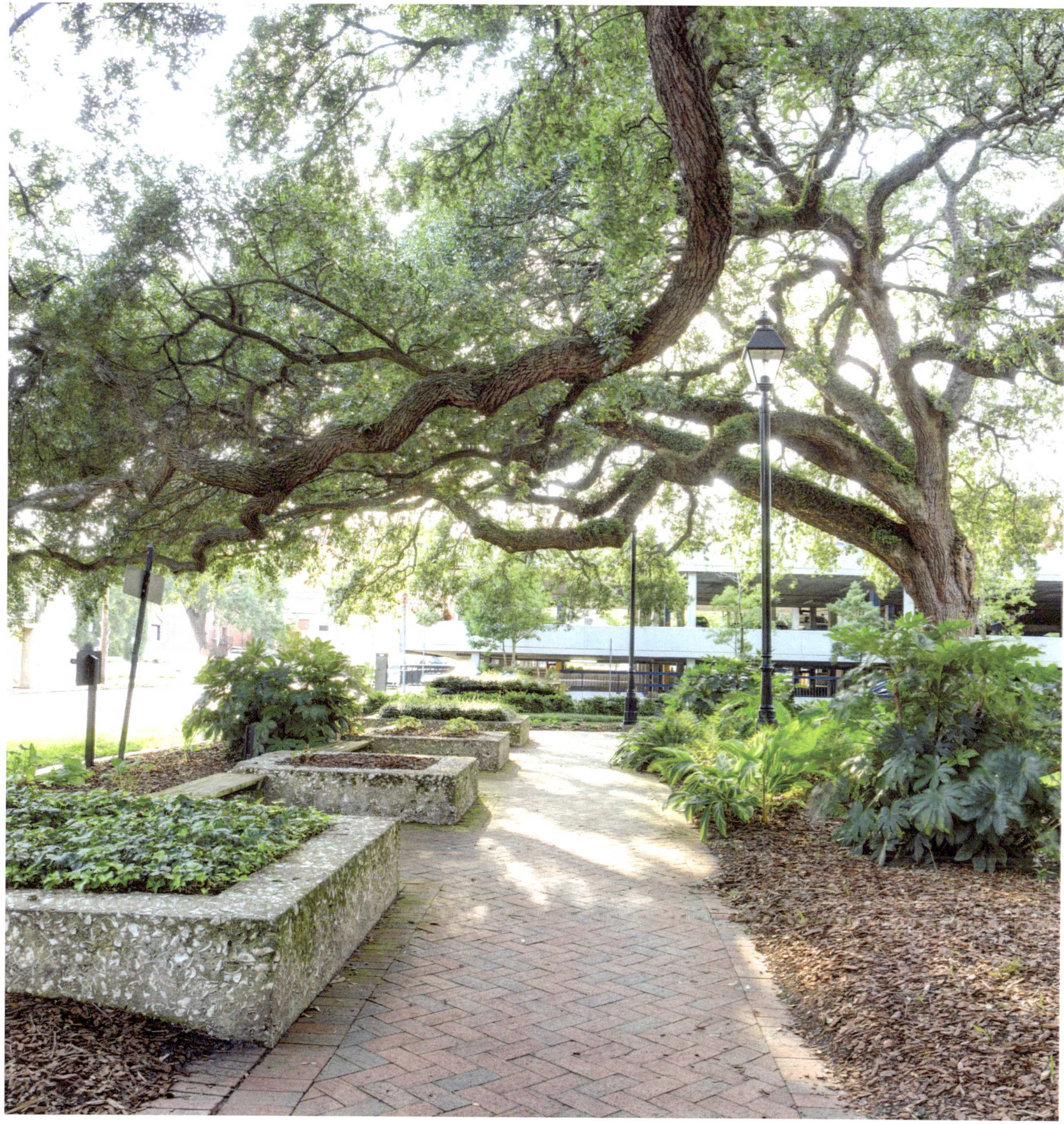

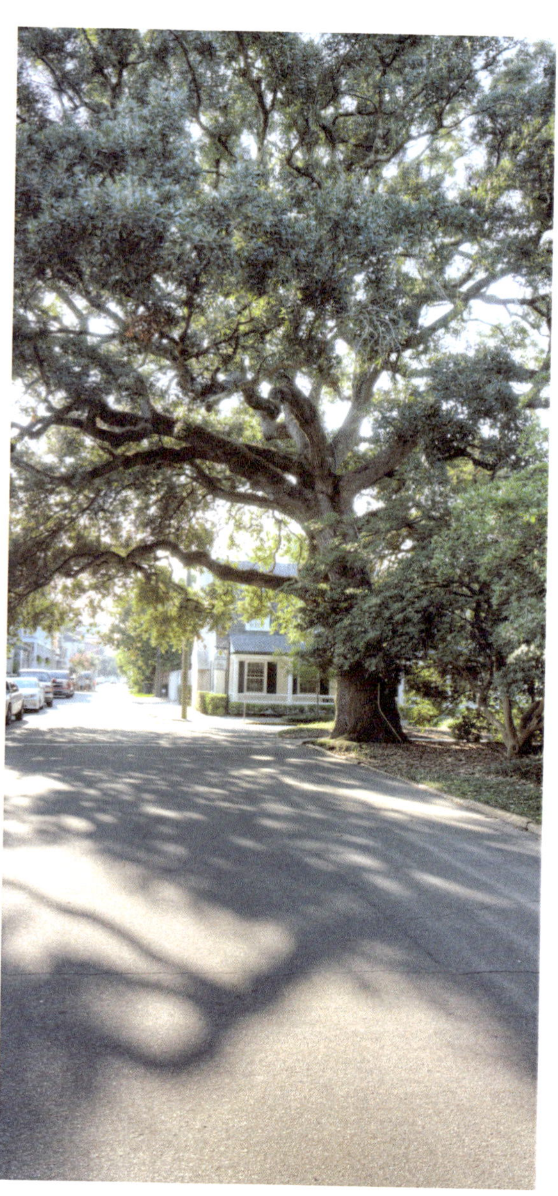

Remembering the days when but a small child,
Feeling adventure was waiting for me,
Run with abandon into the wild,
Amazed at how much there was left to see.

A world of beauty and a world of joy,
Ceaseless mysteries to be discovered;
Building dream castles you cannot destroy,
Rich treasures awaiting to be uncovered.

Childhood is not just a time for the young,
It's a sense we must long prize and preserve.
It is never merely the songs we have sung,
But the music we yet hear and deserve.

There is no grown-up act we may do
That makes the phrase "I am a child" untrue.

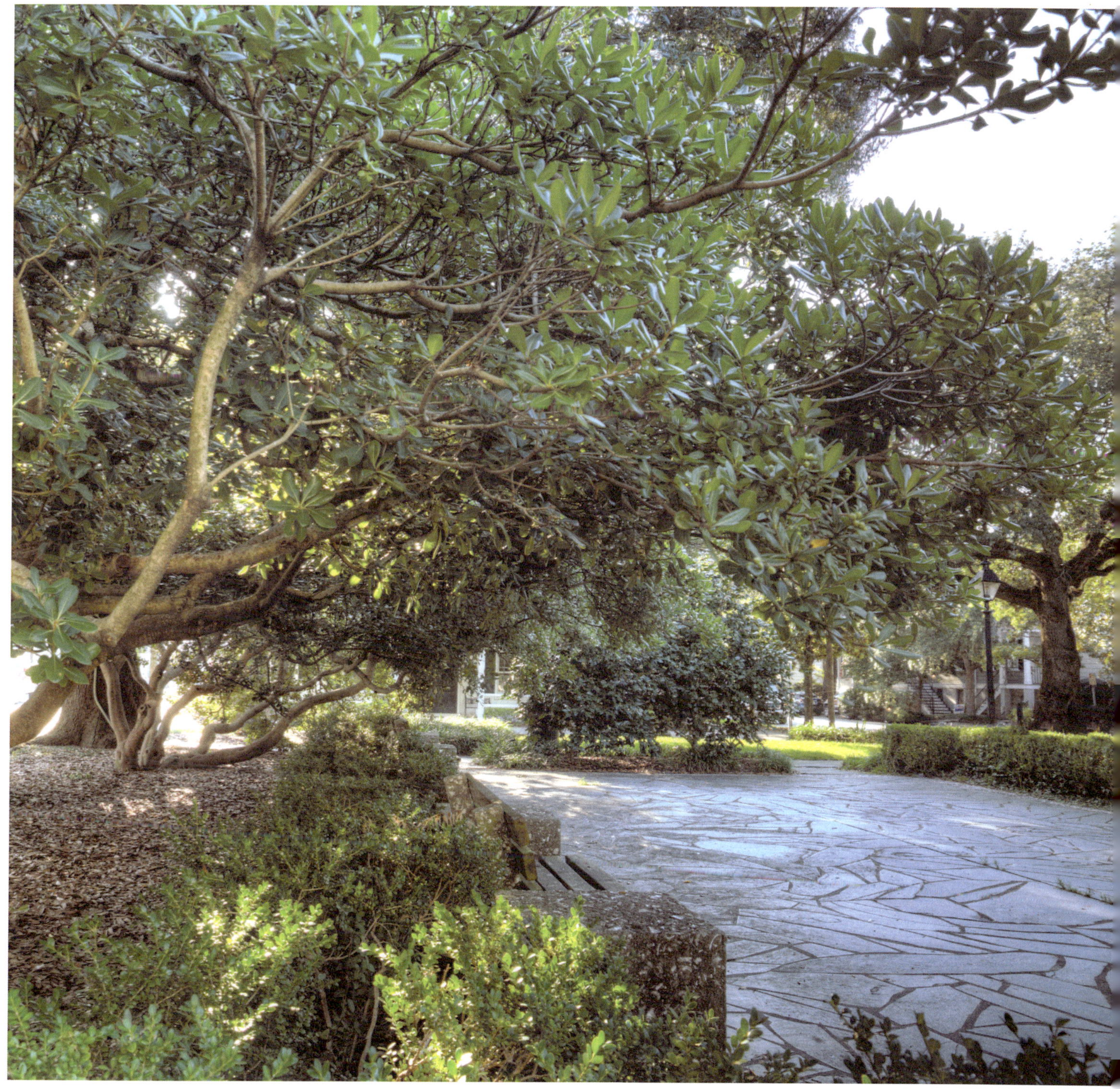

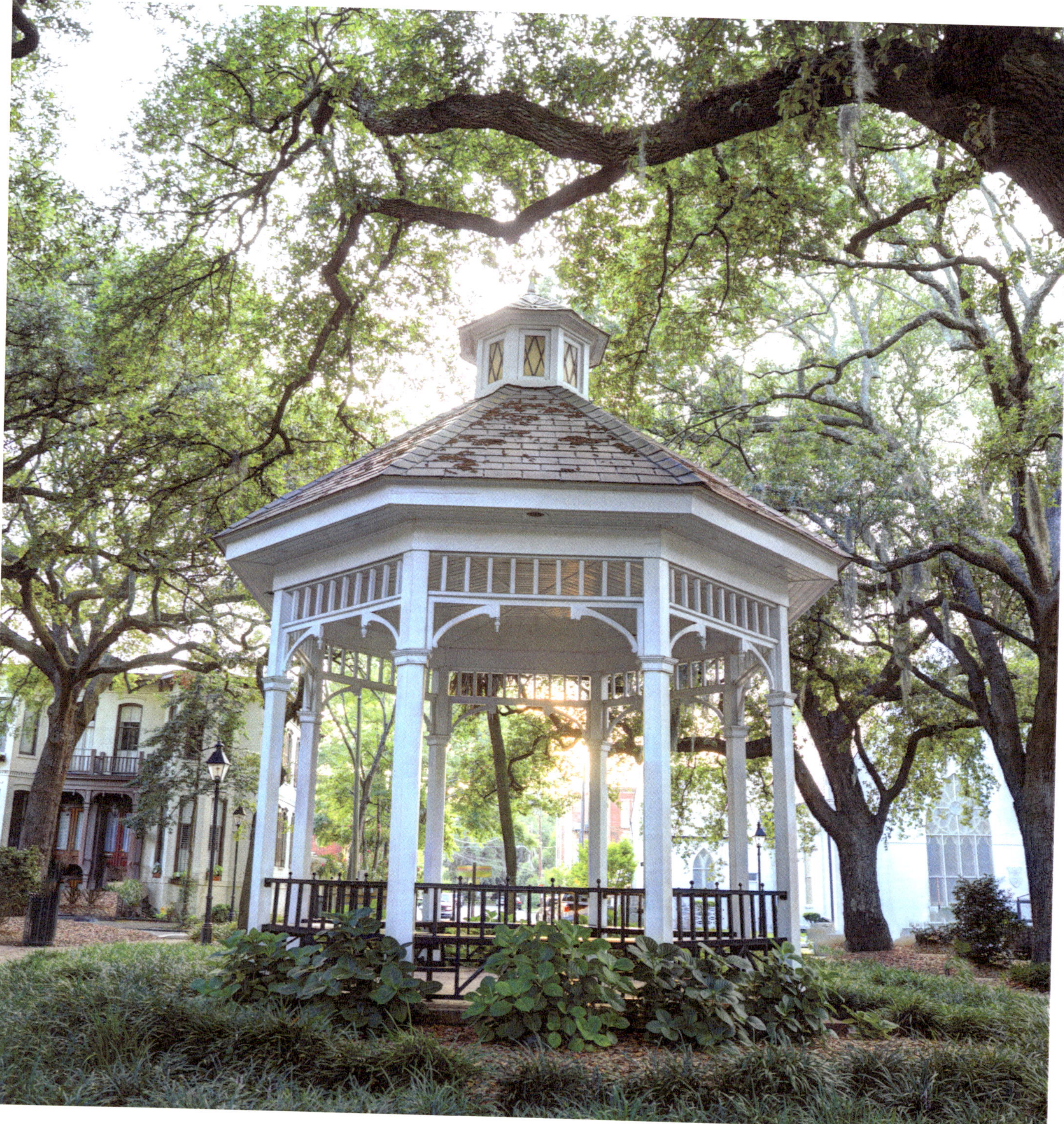

Whitefield Square

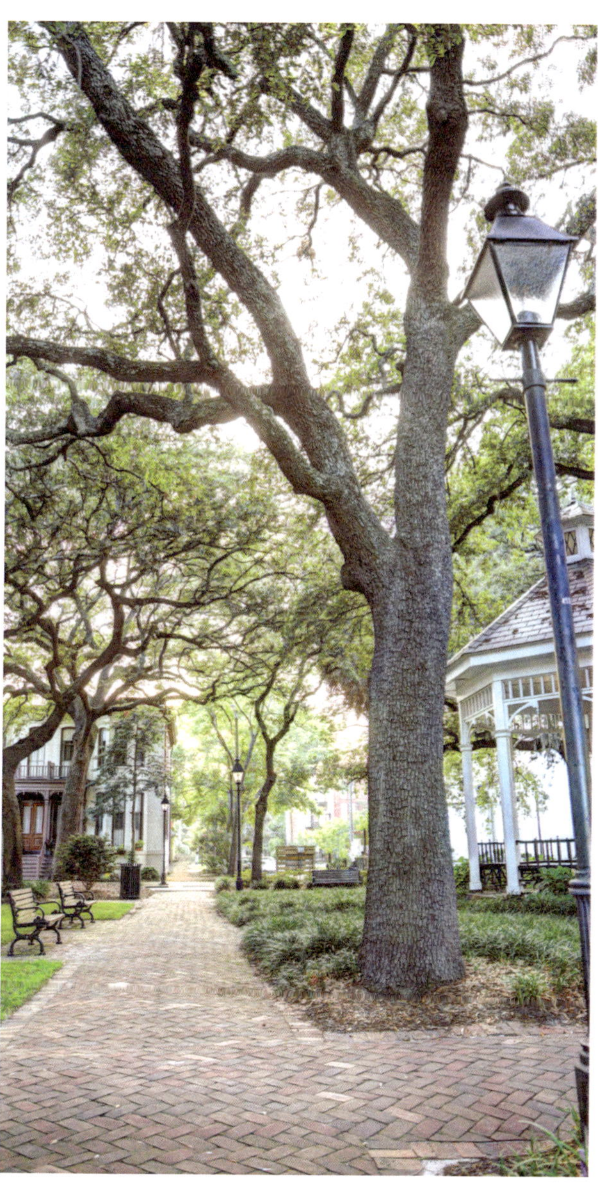

They meet in the square, near to be wed,
The groom in a suit, the bride in a gown,
Her hands hold flowers of white and red,
The shadows grow long as the sun goes down.

How often this square hears old and new vows?
How many families together it's brought?
Who may be planning their wedding day now?
How many ancestors shan't be forgot?

Embrace the beloved and each loving moment,
The lives that begin and are laid to rest there,
Honor past and the future that form our descent,
Perhaps this is why it's a wedding square.

Those near and far cross the world to see
This sacred place for a Jubilee.

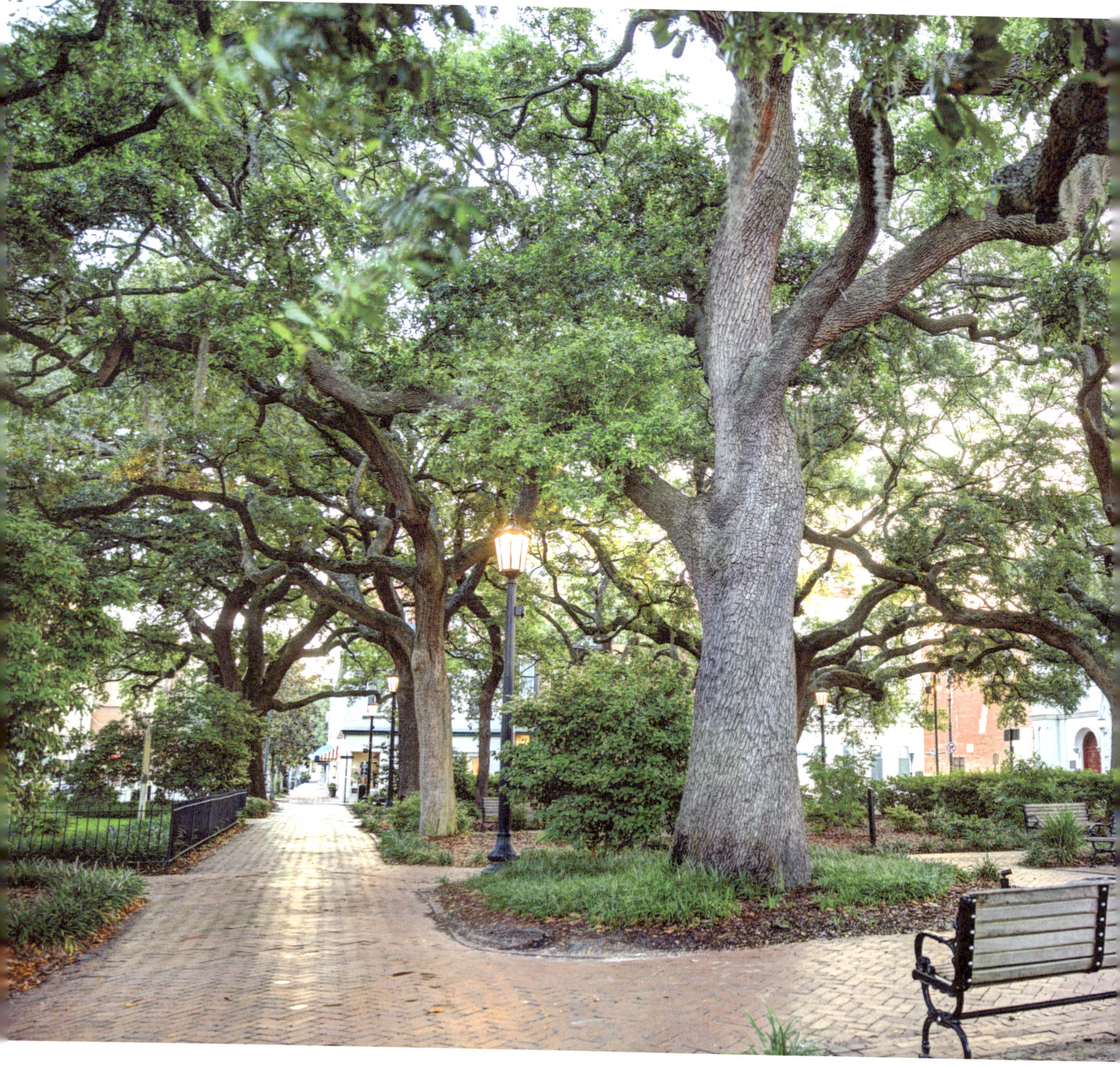

Wright Square

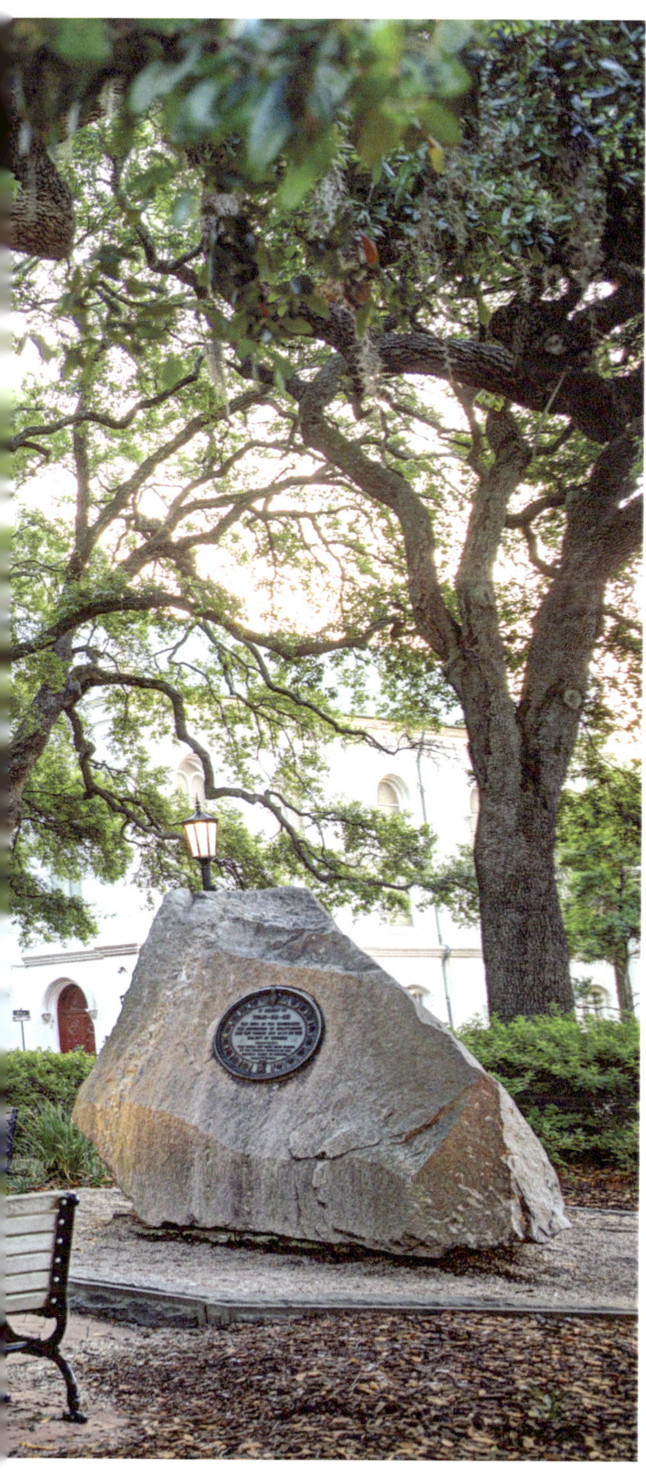

The trees are wise, they know what is true,
Tangled branches weave together the shade;
A large oak witnesses the old and the new,
Leaves whisper hushed secrets that must never fade.

Sit 'neath the canopy and learn what is told,
The stories that only the sagest do know,
The value of which is greater than gold,
The histories and tales from long ago.

This treasure of knowledge is there to be gained,
The lessons of yore and yet how to be
Free from fear and sorrow and pain,
By meditating under an old scraggly tree.

Aim we must live like the grand ancient oak,
Knowing that time is reality's smoke.

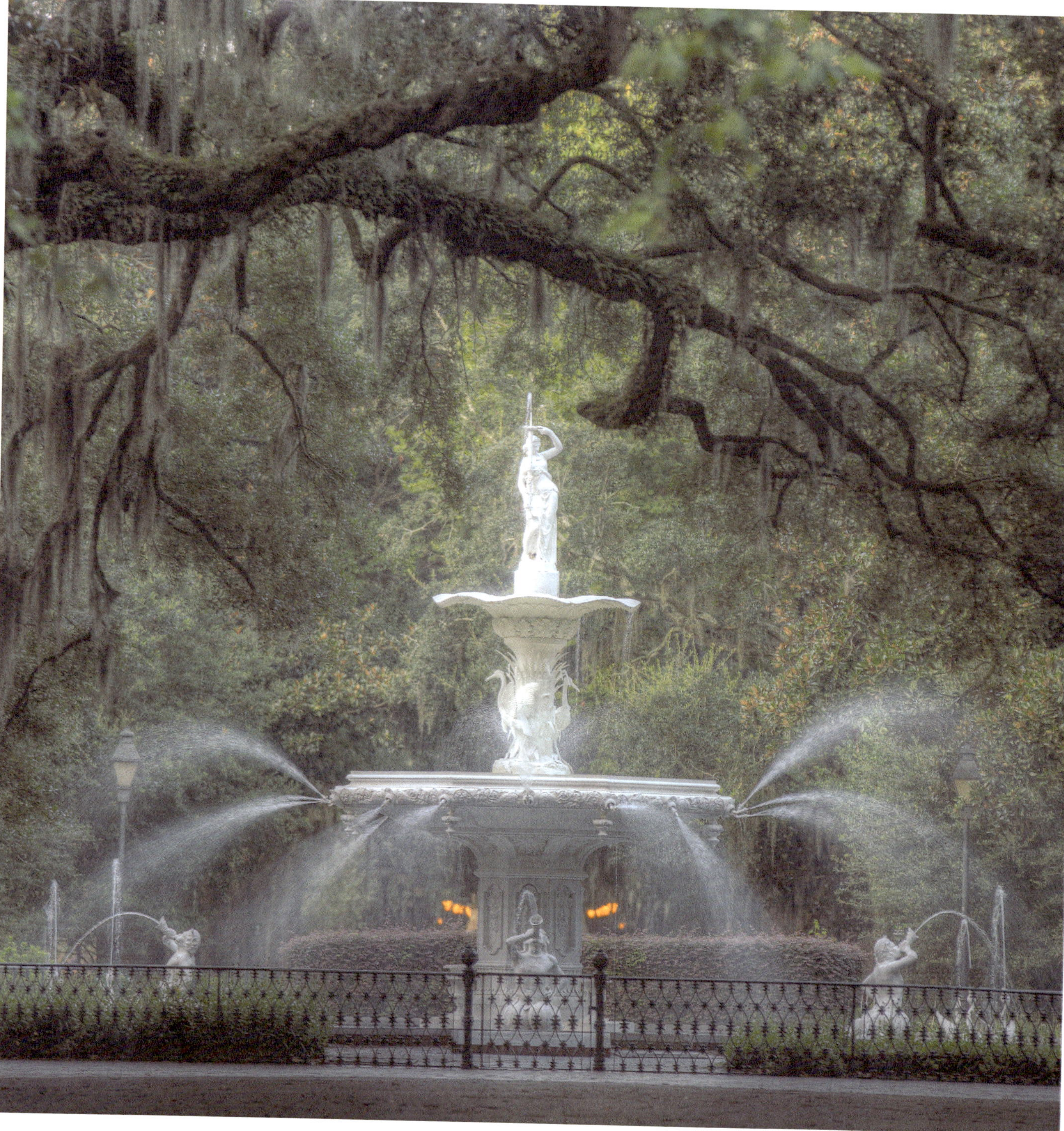

Forsyth Park

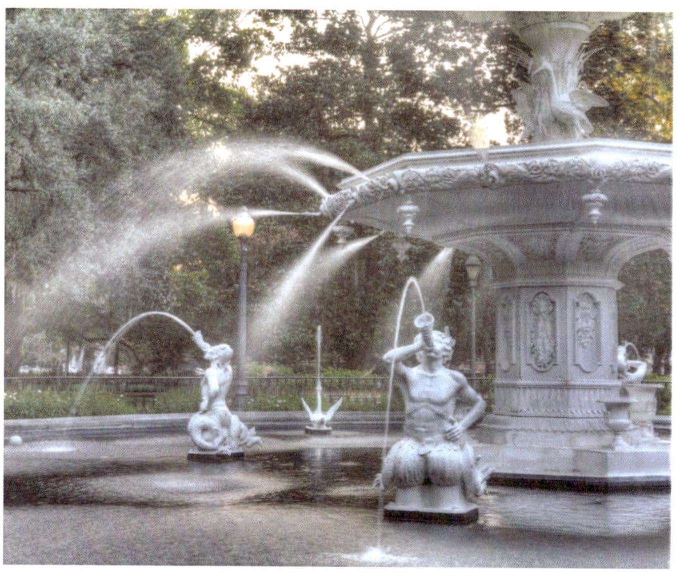

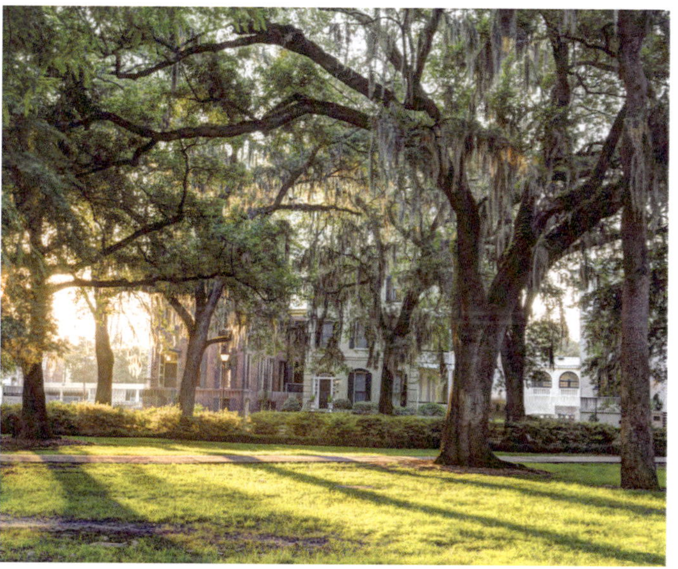

Verdant memories flow through my head,
Sun shines in my mind from some yesterday;
Each night when I finally climb into bed,
I listen to what these memories do say.

They say I should dance and laugh and play more,
They say to set free all my striving and stress,
They say don't just walk but that I should soar,
Be loving and gracious and find much to bless.

Days of gold ere I spent lacing a memory,
Nights of silver are saved building new dreams,
Time's value is hidden, a harbor of synergy,
Moments have costs in their fleeting regimes.

Tread tenderly 'cross the fertile soil,
Let love take root with much room to grow,
Let limbs spread around this mortal coil,
Embrace with kindness all you will know.

The soul is a garden that must be tended,
The world's inhabitants buds to be friended.

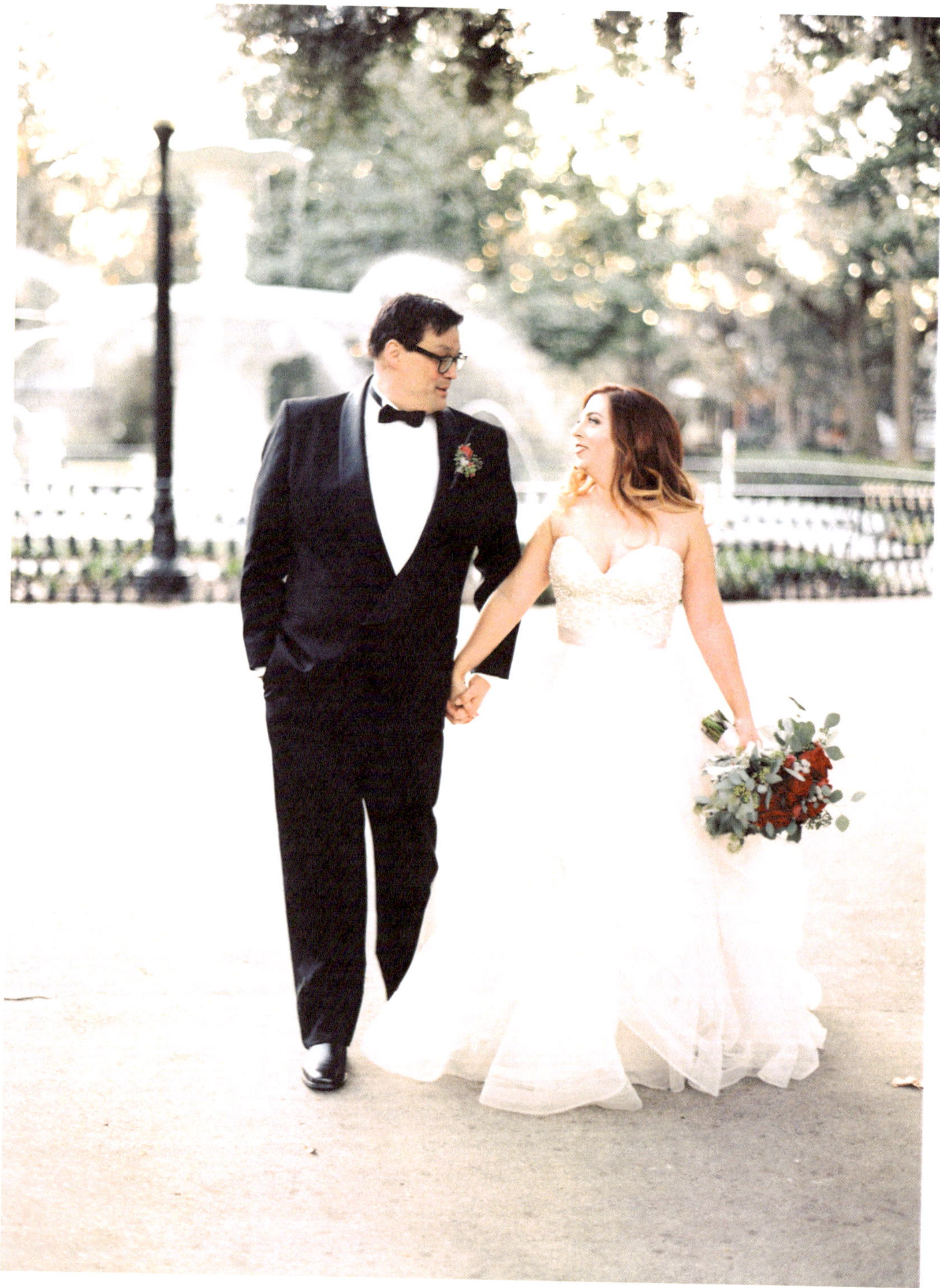

About the Authors

In 2018, Megan Jones and Christopher Soucy were married in Forsyth Park in front of Savannah's iconic fountain.

These two creatives — known locally and beyond for their ongoing support of the arts — then decided to combine their talents and craft this book as an ode to their love of Savannah and the city's past, present, and posterity.

Megan hails from Northbrook, Illinois, and a family of artists. After moving to Savannah to study at SCAD, she first applied her passion for photography to the business of matrimony, helping others capture cherished memories of their weddings and elopements.

With a deep appreciation of aesthetics, her repertoire and reputation has continued to expand.

Her landscapes (of her new home and beyond) are iconic, and in 2017, she launched Savannah Glamour — a female-focused studio that specializes in glamour, pinup, and boudoir portraiture and encourages women to see themselves in a different, gentler light against the most beautiful backdrops Savannah has to offer.

Savannah Glamour has won awards for the "Best Portrait Studio," and Megan has been recognized as one of the top boudoir photographers in the South and the world.

Turning her philogyny and camera toward the Hostess City of the South, Megan photographed all the squares of Savannah.

These alluring images then provided the inspiration for the poems in these pages, through which Christopher Soucy weaves aspects of the past and the present specific to each square.

Christopher is a playwright, poet, and screenwriter who settled in Savannah after a stint in the army.

An eclectic storyteller, his tales span the genres of mystery, detection, comedy, satire, and the supernatural. He is also known for his theater projects such as Odd Lot Improv.

Like Megan, Christopher can be found out and about in Savannah, contemplating the then and the now and shaping both old tales and new.

His work draws from literature, life, history, a love of humanity, and certain idiosyncratic phobias (that may or may not involve clowns and haberdashery).

Uniting both the personal and the professional, Megan's portraiture and Christopher's poetry capture life's ephemeral and enduring moments in art.

Emotion and color, light and words, time and place … whether for visitor or resident, the squares of Savannah embolden and abide.

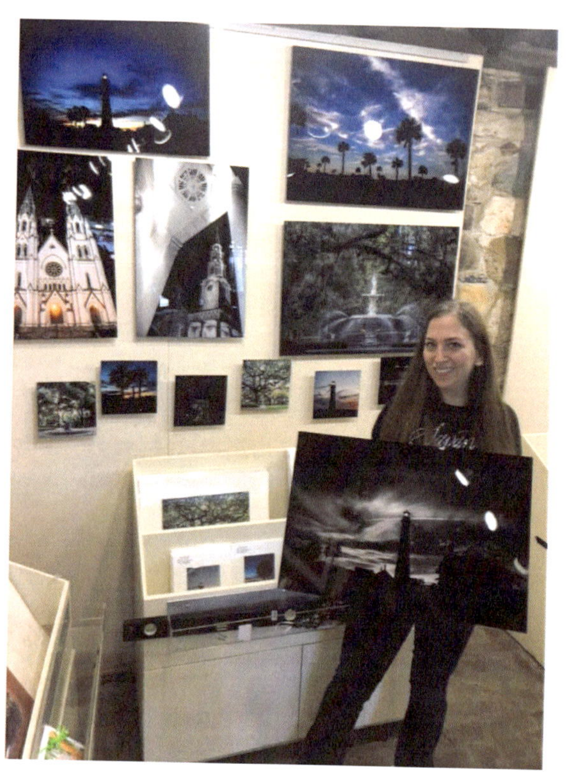

Reprints of individual photographs in various formats (prints, metals, canvases) are available for purchase.

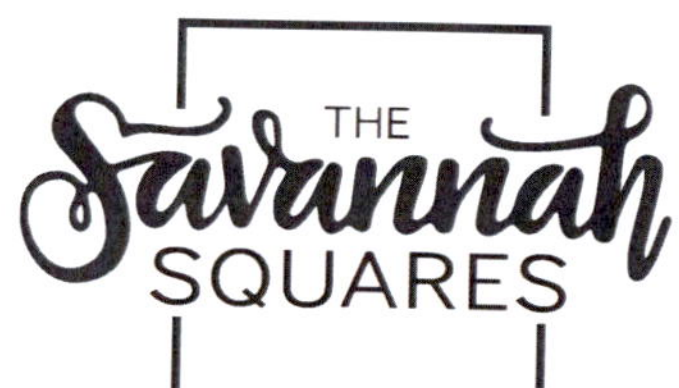

www.TheSavannahSquares.com

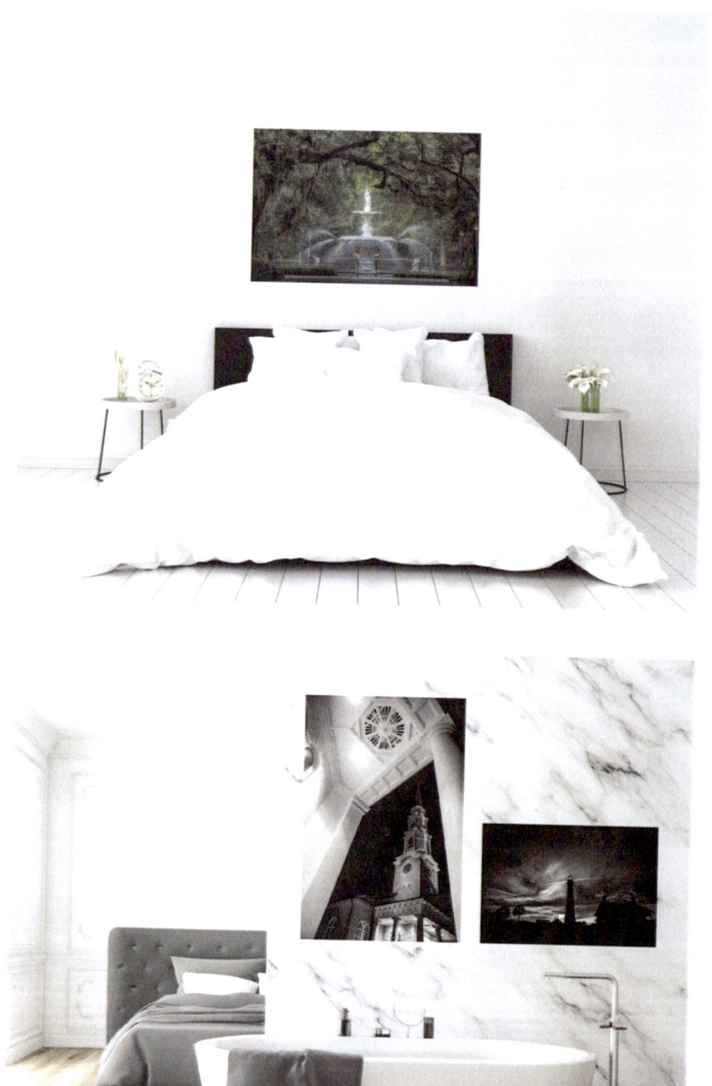

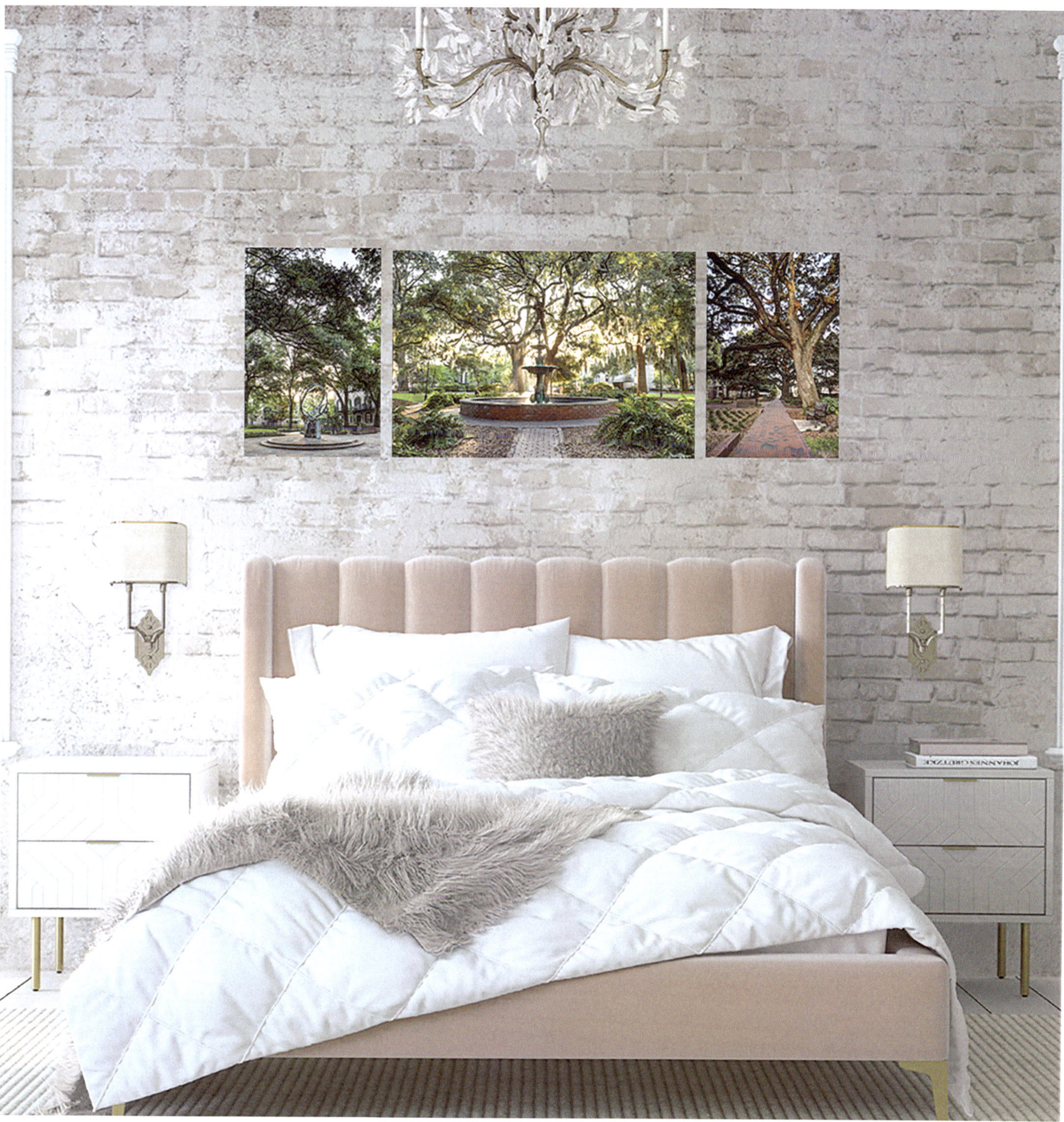

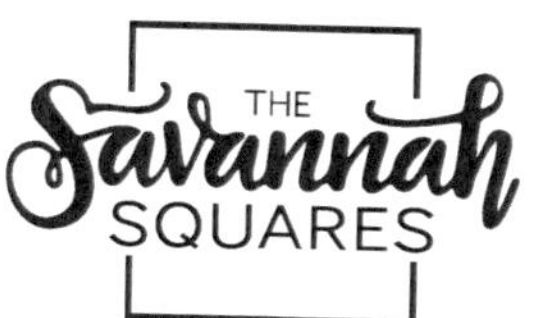

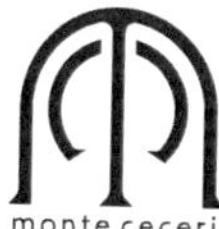